Lilac Dreams

My Journey from a Sewer Drain to the Boardroom

Bonnie C. Hathcock

Print Edition ISBN 978-0692783245

Lilac Dreams: My Journey from a Sewer Drain to the Boardroom by Bonnie C. Hathcock. —1st ed.

www.bonniehathcock.com

*Dedicated to my mom, Lola, who stepped into the shadows
so I could have a better life.*

*To my beloved Aunt Bertie and Uncle Clarence, who raised me
with the greatest love and devotion.*

*To my brother, Mike, whom I will always cherish for his
gentle strength and kind heart.*

To my sister, Susan, my dearest and best friend.

*And, most especially, my beloved husband, Lee,
who is my rock and my life.*

Contents

Foreword

Bonnie Hathcock personifies grit. Her father suffered psychological trauma in World War II and abandoned the family when she was three and her brother was six months old. Everything the family owned was repossessed, "right down to the toys."

For a lot of people, a start like this would be a reason not to try, or an excuse not to do well. But with Bonnie and her indomitable spirit, it was about overcoming obstacles. She was inspired by the people who raised her, by her teachers, and by her own dreams. As she says, "We grew up with a strong work ethic, a good set of values and, above all else, a lot of love."

That love grounded her in believing who she could become. Those values and that work ethic carried Bonnie through a distinguished business career. She recently retired from Humana Inc., where she served as the chief human resources officer and senior vice president. Prior to that, she held senior HR positions at US Airways and Siemens. Her many career honors include being named one of the Top 25 Women in Human Resources, Human Resources Executive of the Year, and a Fellow of the National Academy of Human Resources.

During her career, Bonnie was often the only woman in the room with other senior executives. Over and over again, she found herself fighting for results others considered of lesser importance in a hard-nosed business.

When she retired, Bonnie wrote this book to inspire people, perhaps you or someone you love, who feel they've been stopped by life. She shows how a mix of determination and resolve can bring you success, no matter what situation you are in right now.

Bonnie dreamed big, back there on the fire escape of the old apartment building in Shippensburg, Pennsylvania, where she grew up. She boldly confronted her own emotional vulnerabilities and rose to every challenge with a generous spirit.

Michael B. McCallister
Chairman and CEO, Humana Inc. (retired)

Preface

I am not a famous person, but I am a determined person.

In a small town in south central Pennsylvania in the 1950s and 1960s, filled with determination and inspired by dreams, I rose from humble beginnings to the highest ranks of a Fortune 100 corporation and to the top of my field in human resources.

This is the unvarnished story of my early life, with its mistakes and stumbles in youth, and the lessons learned. From the age of three, I was endlessly learning lessons of forgiveness, backbone, generosity and, most importantly, how to believe in myself.

Through my stories of family, friends and teachers, I share my missteps and difficulties, and how they taught me to be a better person.

I share to show you that when we are young, we make mistakes. We make mistakes because we're exploring who we are. We're discovering who we can be.

I share to show you that we are not defined by those past mistakes. Despite our different life situations, every one of us has *unique* abilities and talents, and we can all learn to believe in ourselves. In so doing, we can learn to believe in others and help them in their life's journey.

I write this book because I believe that every soul is sacred. You matter. You're important. And if I can help you learn from what I've experienced growing up, my own life will fulfill an important purpose.

I encourage you to dream big dreams. Because if I can do it, you can do it.

It takes hard work, courage, steadfastness, and a loving, open heart. And one more thing: It takes faith. Faith as small as a mustard seed will change your life in glorious ways.

I encourage you to keep your dreams alive—and believe.

—Bonnie C. Hathcock

Prologue

The gentle squeak of the green-and-white gliders broke the silence of the quiet evening. On what seemed like an endlessly beautiful summer night, Aunt Bertie and I sat gliding away on the back porch of the old, second-floor apartment in Pennsylvania, where she had raised me. The squeak of those familiar chairs added a soothing calm to the already tranquil night.

As we drifted along in the still night air, the only other sound we heard was the television my husband Lee was watching inside as he relaxed after a long day.

And the crickets. The sound of the crickets in Miss Nancy's yard next door. At least, it had been Miss Nancy's yard when I was a child. When she died, a bank bought her stately home and gardens which, thankfully, the bank preserved. Hers were the lush, green gardens of my youth. Oh, how my dreams were inspired by her gardens in days past. Sitting here now on the back porch, enjoying the warm night air, my heart rejoiced at once again being near her sumptuous grass and the commanding trees so carefully etched in my memory.

Earlier that day, my alma mater, Shippensburg University, had awarded me one of its top honors: Distinguished Alumnus. Lee and I had flown in only the previous day on the corporate jet to attend the awards ceremony. As I sat there with Bertie that night, I was still trying to grasp the reality of receiving such an award from this respected Pennsylvania university.

Bertie broke the silence. "I was worried about you today. When you went up there to make your speech, I worried that you would forget what you wanted to say. You didn't have any notes."

"I know," I said.

I knew she was remembering the time when I was eight and forgot the lines to the poem I was reciting for her Sunday School class banquet. All eyes had been on me that night as I stumbled and bumbled the beginning of my presentation. "I'm sorry," I had said to the class. "I've forgotten it. I've just forgotten it."

There was no reason on Earth I should have forgotten that poem. I had walked around our apartment for weeks, reciting it over and over. I knew it cold. But when I got up front that night, I froze. My fears grabbed hold of me, and I couldn't remember the first line—or any line—of my well-rehearsed poem. Both Bertie and I were humiliated. Plumb humiliated.

"I know," I repeated to Bertie as we sat on the gliders, this night in 2002. "But Bertie, it's been a long time since I forgot that poem."

She nodded, and we continued to glide.

"I never get up in front of people anymore without being prepared," I continued. "You see, for today, I prepared my remarks and held them in my head and heart. I knew every word I was going to say. Just like that time you're remembering. Only *this* time, I had had lots more practice." I smiled.

She took a short pause. "Well, you did good."

A compliment from Bertie meant the world to me. She had raised me since I was three, going on four. She had loved me with a mother's love, and I had loved her back just as much. Bertie's influence in my life was immeasurable. Her faith, her love, her guidance. She set high standards and expected me to live up to them, but she loved me more than she loved herself. Her heart was pure gold. I adored her.

No longer conscious of the television in the distance, I heard only the crickets and the pleasing squeak of the gliders. I felt so honored. Bertie thought I had done well. I soaked in her compliment.

Finally, she broke the silence again. "But you told them in your talk that we didn't have any money," she said quietly. As she said it, she looked over at me and searched my eyes for the reason I had said that.

Impulsively, I replied, "But, Bertie, we didn't have any money. We didn't have any money to send me to college."

She replied in a calm voice, "But you kids had anything you wanted. We made sure of that."

I heard the hurt in her voice. She was right. Bertie, her husband—whom we called Dad, even though he wasn't our real father, and our mom had made sure my brother and I never wanted for anything. We had new school clothes each year from the five and dime where Bertie worked, a pantry chock full of good food, and a swing set cemented in concrete so we could soar.

Most of all, we had love. Love filled our hearts and our home.

Yes, Bertie was right. We had never wanted for anything.

She reminded me of the true meaning of abundance as we sat gliding to the comforting sound of the crickets and the gentle squeak of the gliders. We had everything of value life could offer.

Bertie was dear to me, and I had hurt her. I was deeply touched and sorry. I thought long and hard about her words as we sat together there in the security of the old screened porch.

"We did have everything, Bertie. We truly did."

If only I could do my talk all over again.

We then turned to other topics and just enjoyed our time together. A little later, as we both grew quiet, I began to think again about the gardens below in Miss Nancy's yard. A bittersweet ache came over me as I reflected on what those gardens had meant to me. They were the object of my dreams. No, we didn't have a lot of money, but we were rich in love. The security of love had fueled my dreams—dreams of a life when one day I, too, could have a garden.

My mind wandered back to how it all began as I sat there on that warm summer night, gliding with my beloved Bertie.

Childhood

Lilac Dreams

I grew up on Main Street in Shippensburg, Pennsylvania. Actually, that's the colloquial name. The real name is King Street. Uncle Clarence, who raised me, always used the informal names for streets. Like so many things I do the way they taught me, I use the informal street names throughout this book.

Even though we lived in a simple apartment, we were surrounded by enormous wealth. Some of our town's most privileged residents lived next door and just down the street from our brick apartment building. Their impressive homes lined Main Street on both sides. Collectively, they formed a millionaire's row.

There were the prosperous Stewarts, a family of Scots-Irish Presbyterians with elite educations. Some were doctors, others prominent businessmen. Doc Stewart owned the two homes cattycornered from us. The brick home—painted white with dark-green trim—had been converted into his doctor's office. Next door to his office sat the handsome limestone home with its snowy white trim. This is where he and his wife raised their children, entertained their guests, and maintained their graceful gardens in the back.

Farther west on Main Street was another Stewart home, one of the most regal mansions of the day and reminiscent of the fine estates owned by late-nineteenth-century industrialists. This grand home eventually was converted into the town library.

Then, right next door to our apartment building, was the distinguished and historically significant McLean-McCreary House, which factored prominently into Civil War history. During the war, the house was owned by tanner William McLean, who hid his leather from the Confederate troops by hiding it in false bottoms built into his tanning vats. William's son George, while home from Princeton University, heard a commotion in the street outside the house and went to the front porch to investigate. He saw a Confederate cavalry unit ride by on a mission, and George believed he recognized one of his classmates among them. Shortly thereafter, George enlisted in the Union Army. He was mortally wounded during the battle of Fredericksburg.

On another occasion during the Civil War, Confederate troops were present on Main Street, some resting on the curb and some on the McLean porch. In the group, Mrs. McLean noticed a very young soldier who had a persistent cough. Throughout the evening and during the night, she heard him cough. She felt so sorry for him. In the morning, Mrs. McLean and her daughter Nancy made coffee for the men and gave them slices of homemade bread with apple butter to eat with the steaming coffee. The young boy with the cough was able to move out with the rest of the men when they departed.

Eventually the McLean-McCreary Home would be occupied solely by Miss Nancy McCreary, great granddaughter of William and Nancy McLean. Nancy McCreary had inherited the dignified brick home, with its Georgian architecture and noble white columns, from her mother and father. Her father, Dr. Bruce McCreary, had established his residence and home office there years before. Miss Nancy, as we respectfully called her, was a professor of English literature at Shippensburg University. She retired when I was around 10 years old. She lived alone in the ancestral home.

My only glimpses of the inside of Miss Nancy's home occurred on the few occasions that she was on her front porch with the door open when I passed by. Even though she was talking with a visitor, she always greeted me in her refined and gracious manner. In returning her greeting, I could steal a look inside her home without appearing nosy.

I had never seen such well-born luxury and elegance. Chairs of soft yellow silk and gilded mirrors on the wall filled my imagination for days after those glimpses, with thoughts of what it must be like to live there. With her door open, the cheery tints of yellow and white drenched me in a lighthearted glow.

As breathtaking as her home was on the inside, it was the outside that inspired my dreams. Her garden was magnificent.

From the fire escape leading from the second floor of my apartment building, I had a clear view of Miss Nancy's garden with its luxurious green grass and spring tulips. Resplendent in colors of red, yellow and orange, her tulips flowed bountifully along the narrow concrete path that curved through her garden. Closer to the back, daffodils turned their yellow faces to the sun and contrasted brilliantly with the emerald opulence of the grass. The branches of commanding trees created shade on sunny summer afternoons and an icy wonderland on snowy winter days.

It was under the shade of those majestic trees on balmy summer afternoons that Miss Nancy entertained her friends, who wore finely spun dresses in gossamer shades of yellow, green and pink as she treated them to lemonade in tall glasses served on silver trays.

My view from the fire escape permitted me to take it all in without being noticed. Seeing her with her guests always left me with a bittersweet feeling. Although each event inspired my imagination, I felt a self-inflicted pain of being excluded. But that passed, and I soon enjoyed gazing once again.

A cement wall separated Miss Nancy's garden from the dirt parking lot in back of our apartment building. Her kitchen window was just beyond the cement wall and, sometimes, I would see her washing a few dishes. As she worked, she would look out at the white honeysuckle that grew heartily on top of the wall. Even from my high perch, I could smell the perfumed scent of the lavish vine her gardener had planted many years before. The only signs of disharmony I ever noticed in Miss Nancy's garden were the toy guns and plastic soldiers that belonged to my younger brother, Mikey. I wouldn't have dared enter her garden. I was content merely to look at it. For my little brother, however, the temptation of being in there was just too great. He had to play there.

When he was around four years old, he boldly took the initiative. Standing on his tiptoes, he knocked on Miss Nancy's door and asked if he could play in her garden from time to time. Not only did she grant him permission, she invited him in for iced tea. After that, he felt free to play there periodically.

Over the years, whenever it was time for dinner, I would set out looking for my brother in all the usual places. He would normally be in the dirt parking lot behind our building soaring high on our swing, batting stones, or playing with his toys. When this setting failed to deliver him, I headed to Miss Nancy's back fence and called his name. He would raise his head, gather his playthings, and head for dinner through her back garden gate, over to our side, and up the fire escape to our second-floor apartment. Unlike me, Mikey didn't just dream about a beautiful garden. He experienced its glorious splendor for himself.

The most alluring part of Miss Nancy's garden for me was her lilac tree. The tree was large and grew disobediently over the garden fence, spilling onto the parking lot. Light purple, it was deliciously scented in a velvety soft perfume, with tiny sculpted petals forming big, lush boughs. From the top step of the fire escape, I could enjoy Miss Nancy's lilacs for weeks on end. And, for those few brief weeks each spring, they were my lilacs, as well.

To smell the heavenly fragrance, all I had to do was pull one of the errant boughs to my nose. In an instant, my senses were filled with pure joy. With Miss Nancy's permission, I would clip a few of her lilacs for our spring table.

Even beyond the lilacs, Miss Nancy's garden held a mystery and fascination for the dreamer in me. I wanted a garden of my own one day, where I would serve lemonade on silver trays to ladies in fine dresses. A grand garden filled with tulips and daffodils in the spring, emerald-green grass, and commanding trees that would provide shade in the summer and an icy wonderland in the winter. And lilacs. Beautiful, nostalgic lilacs.

It would be many years and many roadblocks before my dream came true.

Because before there were dreams of lilacs, there was harsh reality.

Before the Lilacs

My father abandoned us abruptly and quietly. He left one day when I was about three years old and stayed gone essentially the rest of my life. His name was Johnny, he was from Nashville, Tennessee, and he suffered psychological trauma in World War II. After that, he became an alcoholic.

My mind's sketchbook of Johnny is made of bits and pieces I've heard from family members. They say he was a decent man, a kind and charming man, and that he had many friends—when he was sober.

Johnny was raised by his Aunt Katy, who sent him to good Catholic schools and made sure he had proper manners. Tall and handsome, he served as an altar boy in his church, and he enjoyed unconditional love from Aunt Katy.

When World War II broke out, Johnny found himself in the middle of the action as a young infantryman. That's when life changed him. It was his first trip away from the South.

Not long after joining the service, he landed on a foreign shore and was thrust into the theater of war. For three long days and nights, he looked into the face of a dead soldier as they both lay trapped in a foxhole somewhere in Europe. He never got over it.

During the Nuremberg Trials in Germany in 1945–1946, Johnny was selected by the United States military to serve as a courtroom guard for the proceedings. Tall and fit, he served honorably.

After his time in battle, he must have wanted to return home to the South. Instead, his orders took him north to Carlisle, Pennsylvania, home of the U.S. Army War College. His experience at Nuremberg had equipped him for a role as a military policeman.

While on guard duty one night, Johnny met my mom on her way to a dance on the base with her sister Janet. Mom had pretty black hair, long and thick, and a winning, red-lipstick smile. Much of Johnny's charm had returned by then, and he courteously introduced himself. His elegant manners and good looks captured her heart. In that moment, she knew she had met the man of her dreams. They got married about a year after Johnny completed his military service and moved to Shippensburg, Pennsylvania, a smaller town twenty-two miles farther south.

Life with Johnny had good times. Everyone fell in love with his politeness and manners, including Mom's large family. Stories abound of how enjoyable it was to visit with my parents in their apartment, in an old house on the crest of a hill. When visitors came, Johnny would run out onto the porch, smiling big, grab them by the elbow, and usher them into his clean-as-a-whistle kitchen for cake and coffee. Johnny loved people.

Eventually, Johnny and my mother, Lola, had two children: me and my little brother, John Michael. They nicknamed him Mikey. Mom described how my father would hold me on his lap for hours, swaying and cooing his baby daughter to sleep and appreciating how God had blessed him. When his son was born two and a half years later, Johnny's joy was complete.

But Johnny was drinking more and more.

Shortly before my brother was born in 1951, Johnny left my fully pregnant mother standing for hours outside the grocery store with her checked-out grocery cart while he rendezvoused with Pearl. While Mom was shopping for groceries and I was home with a babysitter, Johnny was romping with a party girl.

I can only imagine Mom's fear as she stood there, pregnant, alone, and twenty-five miles from home. Her heart must have ached as she searched each passing car for the recognizable face of my father returning to pick her up. After a couple of hours, Johnny finally came back for her.

Then there was the time a few months after Mikey was born when I was awakened by the light in the hallway beaming into the dark bedroom my brother and I shared. Or maybe it was the raised voices.

My father was replacing a light bulb, standing on a ladder while Mom held it steady. They were arguing. Then Mom's soothing voice encouraged me to go back to sleep.

Johnny was drinking even more, and things were beginning to crumble.

People say he was almost two people: loving father and husband when sober, reckless and willful rabble-rouser when drunk.

During a drunken spree, my father and Aunt Janet's husband, Uncle Sam, slashed and cut their way to a jail sentence by destroying clothes at the dry cleaners where my father worked. They spent months in jail.

The day they came home, my little girl cousins and I were waiting on the porch, searching the top of the hill for sight of them. Finally, there they came, suitcases in hand and all smiles, walking swiftly toward us. Shrieking as we ran, we threw our arms around them. From Mom's perspective, Johnny had returned to his wife and family.

But it wasn't long before his demons drove him to more drinking, as he tried to escape a life he couldn't live. And then he left.

Mom probably didn't realize he was gone at first, as he sometimes stayed away for days. Once she realized he wasn't coming home, she fell apart.

Family members came to be with her. Our home felt cold, empty, and like someone had died. An eerie quiet settled over the apartment.

I was sent outside to sit on the porch step with my older cousin, Larry. While he tried to keep me occupied, I kept turning around and looking through the screen door, searching for Mom. They had her off in another room, but I could still hear her crying. I knew, then, the sound of hurt.

No one will ever know the depth of pain Mom suffered from the betrayal of a man who had professed his love for her and his children. The thought of food must have sickened her. A dark fear of losing her home and all that she had must have clawed at her heart and awakened her in the middle of the night.

Mom had reason to fear. She had finished some of her schooling but had no real skills to make a living. It didn't take long for her fears to play out. When the burly men knocked on our door, Mom let them in. Because she couldn't pay her bills, they repossessed our belongings. They gutted our apartment of everything we owned. From the car out front to all of our furnishings and even our toys, they cleaned us out. All of the fears she must have felt came true.

I stood in shock, watching as one of the men shoved my large doll under his armpit while he grabbed sofa pillows, blankets, and whatever else he could get his hands on before he tramped out the door.

Family members often commented throughout the years that having the furniture and car repossessed was hard enough, but removing the children's toys was cruel. We were left with nothing except our clothes.

Once the men were gone, life had to seem brutal and punishing to Mom, as she stared at the bare floors of her empty apartment. With her children's beds disassembled and removed, her cries of despair echoed off the blank walls of what had once been her home.

Mom's anguish pierced her soul. And little did she know that life was about to take even harsher twists and turns.

Railroad Street

The locomotives sputtered, snorted, and heaved as they lumbered past our cement-block apartment building on Railroad Street. The street is formally called Earl Street, but Bertie and Uncle Clarence always used the informal name, and it just seems right because of my memories of the trains. These bloated giants jarred and clanged into our lives at all hours of the day and night, disgorging their greasy stench into our nostrils and onto our walls.

We never got used to them. We just learned how to suspend living until they noisily pushed through on their long journeys north.

If they gave us any fun at all, it was when Mikey, our two girl cousins—aged 8 and 2—and I were out playing on the street and caught a glimpse of a lone brakeman. We would wave and he would wave back, and we would squeal.

Maybe we were squealing because the snaky, hulking body had finally passed through, and life could return to normal.

Normal. Life was anything but normal for Mom, working two jobs back-to-back trying to provide for her children and put food in our stomachs. She lived a harsh and unbending life.

Mom's memories were fresh and raw over losing everything she had. Hurt and fear went with her to work and came home with her after long days and nights. But there was only one way she could go, and that was through. She had two small children who needed her to assure their safety and security.

Aunt Janet gave us a roof over our heads in that tiny apartment on Railroad Street. Not because she had the room. Because she had a big heart. Knowing we had nowhere else to go when our home was gone, she invited us in.

Seven of us slept in one room, lined up wall-to-wall on unmatched and, usually, unmade beds. There was a small kitchen where the cupboards were often empty, a living room with two windows that overlooked the tracks, and a dingy, cramped bathroom.

Our end of Railroad Street didn't offer much to the families who lived there, but at least the rent was cheaper than elsewhere in town. If the trains weren't enough to discourage people, the shady, dark bars scattered up and down the street made living there almost intolerable.

Mom and Aunt Janet were gone most of each day and night, working hard at factory and restaurant jobs. Aunt Janet's husband, Uncle Sam, stayed home with us children during the day.

Barefoot, dressed in a white T-shirt and black trousers, he would step over hassocks as he moved about. He was indifferent to Mikey and me, but at least he provided a form of protection from the roughnecks and drunkards who hung out on Railroad Street.

With Mom and Aunt Janet absent and Uncle Sam indifferent, my little brother Mikey, now a year old and barely walking, was left to fend for himself with his eight-year-old cousin who thought he was cute as a button. She liked to tease him. It began innocently but escalated into a hurtful game of ear pulling.

She probably started gently at first. But then she did it more and more, and harder and harder. And, finally, she separated his ears from his head.

He cried, but she didn't stop. She saw the scabs and dried-up blood from his infected ears, but she didn't stop. Nothing made her stop. Mikey turned to me with his cries of misery. I didn't know much about protecting him; I wasn't even four myself.

We huddled on one of the beds, and I wrapped my arms around him and held him tight while he cried.

We waited for Mom to come home, because we both knew nothing would soothe his hurts like his mother's familiar arms and voice.

My brother was innocent and good-natured, and Mom and Aunt Janet worked long hours. For this reason, the "game" continued way too long.

Then one day, even I was no longer there to comfort him. He was left alone to cry, at the mercy of his cousin.

Sewer Drain

Bertie was Mom's oldest sister, already fourteen when Mom was born. Bertie always held a special place in her heart for my mother. One cold October day, she walked down the stairs from her own spacious, warm apartment on Main Street, crossed to the other side, and walked the half block to the Valley Pride Bakery for doughnuts. She then cut through the back alley to the street that ran alongside our tiny apartment on Railroad Street.

Bertie had recently left a job she had held for more than twenty years at the shirt factory. She was taking a much-needed break before she looked for another job. It was just Bertie and her husband, and he held a good job at the furniture factory in town. With only the two of them, one income could supply their needs for a while if they were careful about their spending. Bertie liked having a little freedom to do things, like go visit her younger sister who was now living on Railroad Street.

Most days, Mikey and I and our cousins could see Aunt Bertie coming from our window above the tracks. During the cold months, she wore a green corduroy swing coat with its flared silhouette creating emerald waves as she walked. Often, she carried a white Valley Pride Bakery bag filled with a half-dozen plain cake and cinnamon-sugared doughnuts for us children. We always liked seeing Bertie heading toward us.

That October day, however, no one was watching from the window.

As Bertie got closer to our apartment building, she saw a small child playing alone in the sewer drain. *Why, that child is no more than a baby!* she thought in alarm and rushed into the street, which was busy with passing cars and trains that went by at all hours.

As Bertie got closer, she saw that the child was me, and I wasn't wearing a coat on that cold day.

She hurried to my side and noticed I had only one button buttoned on my thin dress, was wearing no shoes, and my hair was uncombed. It looked to Bertie as if I had dressed myself.

It didn't take her long to figure out that my mother was away working and I was unsupervised out here on the street. Emotions washed through her. She was moved by memories of her own little boy, who died shortly after she gave birth. She was moved by her love for children.

The next thing I knew, I was soaking in a hot, sudsy tub, getting my hair washed and then being taken uptown for new dresses, shoes, and a coat. It all happened so fast.

That night, I found myself with a tummy full of good cooking, in a bedroom lit by a soft pink lamp. Under the comforting glow of the lamp, Bertie read to me from a thick, strange book. Bertie was a strong woman of great faith, and her significant influence in my life began that very night. Her words were soothing, and I got drowsy in the warmth of the snuggly blankets and the pink gentleness of the cozy room. I felt safe and protected.

Before I drifted off to sleep that night, I thought, *This must be Hollywood. This must be that nice place they all talk about.*

The only problem was that my brother Mikey was still at Railroad Street, with little food and no protection. And I missed my mother.

But I was never to return to Railroad Street. At almost four years old, I had a new home.

At least, I thought I did.

Life Interrupted

I felt sick as I sat on the big chair in Aunt Bertie's living room, my feet barely reaching the end of the seat cushion. All I could do was stare: stare at my black patent leather shoes and lacy white anklets.

Bertie gave me my bath, curled my dark hair into Shirley Temple ringlets, and dolled me up in a frilly dress. I was waiting for my mother and brother. We were headed south to Tennessee.

Somehow, Johnny had persuaded my mom to try again, only this time in his home city of Nashville. In the year since he had left, Mom had struggled to make ends meet, and she was losing the battle. Vulnerable and still in love with her Southern man, she agreed to rejoin him and bring us children, too. Long hours working two jobs and living in a crowded apartment not her own had worn her down. And I had been taken away to stay with Bertie and Uncle Clarence on Main Street. It was all too much for Mom. Even though her life with Johnny had been difficult and uncertain, life was unkind and unbearable without him.

So there I sat, in my wonderful and safe new home with Bertie and Uncle Clarence, feeling sick and sad, and fighting tears. I wanted to throw up. I dreaded leaving.

I was too young to realize that no one had actually decided if this was my "forever" home, besides me. I assumed it. It felt so right.

Here, I could play all day with Aunt Bertie's knickknacks. The ceramic stagecoach and driver were my favorites, and they took me across prairies and mountains without ever leaving the living room or underneath the coffee table, for that matter. Here, I ate good, hot meals and slept in a quiet, cozy bedroom. Here, I had new toys, books, and everything a four-year-old could ever need.

By now, my father was fading from my life. He had been gone for almost a year, and the love of my aunt and uncle was becoming my new normal. I was moving on.

Mom, on the other hand, was fighting. She was fighting hard to re-build her life.

From the time she was born, Mom was a survivor. She weighed less than two pounds at birth. The kindly old doctor who delivered her looked down at her lying in the palms of his hands and knew what to do, because he had seen other "blue babies" before. "Clean this one up for burial," he told his nurse. "She won't make it."

Mom was a twin. Her big sister, Beulah—who was nicknamed Bootie—was born just moments before her, healthy and robust. As the nurse lifted the tiny, two-pound infant from the doctor's hands, she braced herself for the sad task ordered by the physician. Instead of preparing a newborn for her mother's bosom, she would be preparing this one for the undertaker.

She moistened a soft cloth with warm water and began to wash the baby's arms, legs, and face.

And that's when God stepped in. As she dabbed at the infant's mouth, the lifeless baby began to suck on the washcloth. "Why," the nurse loudly exclaimed, "this baby's not sick. She's hungry!"

And with that and lots of nourishment, tiny Lola began her journey to becoming a healthy baby. From that time forward, the family called Lola by her nickname, Tiny. From that time forward, Mom was a survivor.

And now her struggle was almost insurmountable. She would come home from work at night to find her small son crying, both from hunger and sore ears. The bullying had not stopped and those often-empty cupboards on Railroad Street were becoming even emptier. There were so many mouths to feed on so little money. The money that came in paid the rent on the apartment.

But one night, it got to be too much for Mom. Around midnight, she bundled my brother Mikey in blankets and headed out in the darkness of Railroad Street toward Bertie's apartment several blocks away. Mikey was crying, and Mom was crying as she ran with him in her arms.

She carried him up Railroad Street, past the drunks leaning on walls and collapsed in stairwells, past dark alleys with sinister shadows. Finally, the town square. She took a sharp left, crossed the highway, and continued running down Main Street to the unlocked door of her sister's apartment building. She stepped into the warm hallway, ran up the steep flight of stairs with a strength she didn't know she had, and rang Bertie's doorbell.

No one ever came late at night, so Bertie wondered who could be arriving at this hour. When she opened the door, standing there crying was her sister, with her eighteen-month-old son wrapped in blankets in her shaking arms.

All the while, I was sleeping in a quiet, cozy bedroom.

"I could not put my baby to sleep another night without food," Mom pleaded to her sister. "Will you please give him something to eat?"

Bertie did what she always did. She gave generously. Good-hearted Bertie had given generously all of her life, despite difficult circumstances. When she was thirteen, she was stricken with spinal meningitis that left her back deformed. With her ribs stacked one on another, and a gaping cavern in her side, she walked noticeably bent over.

She had enjoyed a perfect body her first thirteen years. Suddenly, she was crippled for life. The kids in school called her "camel," and she felt the sting of that label for many years. As time went on, though, she chose not to notice the uncensored rudeness of others as they stared at her deformed back. It was just something she accepted.

Bertie was disadvantaged, but she never thought of herself as disabled. She worked as hard, or harder, than any able-bodied person. She didn't shy away from long hours, either. She had just completed twenty-plus years at the local shirt craft doing piecework for cents on the dollar. And she would eventually complete another twenty-plus years of standing on her feet at a cash register at the local five and dime in the town square.

To those who loved her, Bertie was not deformed. Anyone who knew her fell in love with her kindness and sharp wit. With only a limited education, she was smart as a whip and had razor-sharp insight. Her penetrating Olivia de Havilland dark eyes could see through the cleverest schemes, like when I tried to get out of my chores by professing too much homework. She could deftly identify fact from fiction.

She'd often be sitting with a ball of yarn in her lap and crochet hooks in her large, farm-tough hands, rocking away in her big chair in the living room while watching Arthur Godfrey on television. She'd look up at Arthur on the tv, then look up at me with those penetrating eyes that signaled she wasn't buying my scheme, and not miss a hook.

So the night Mom came to the door with my brother Mikey, Bertie responded with her usual generosity. The Christian matriarch of her big family of ten brothers and sisters, she always gave generously, even if it hurt.

After a hot meal, Mom bundled Mikey in his blanket and trudged back to Railroad Street, where she slept with him in a cramped bedroom until it was time to get up and go to work. Leaving him unprotected and hungry.

So, when my father called, Mom could not say no.

And now the doorbell was ringing once again. This time, taking me from my quiet and safe new home.

Uprooted

On her husband's thin promises, Mom uprooted all of us and the three of us boarded the train for Nashville.

She did her best to keep Mikey and me well-mannered and entertained on the long trip from south central Pennsylvania to north central Tennessee. All the while, she was afraid to be too hopeful, and she was too in love not to be.

Her wounds were still raw and open from losing Johnny, her home, and all she had. Had he changed? She hoped so.

Since he had left, her children had been split up and there had been talk of sending Mikey and me to the Scotland School for Veterans' Children, an orphanage not far away in Pennsylvania. Times were tough, and Mom saw no way to properly provide for her children and keep them together. If necessary, she would give them up to provide them a better life, a life she couldn't give them on so little income. And while Bertie and her husband Clarence were helping out by letting me stay there, she couldn't expect them to raise her children. Bertie and Clarence had struggled to make ends meet like everyone else. It was true they had it easier than us, but they were a working-class couple like many others.

Now, as she cradled my two-year-old brother in her arms and lay my head against her, Mom's fears of losing us took center stage in her mind during that long trip.

And she worried about something else. Could she be enough for Johnny? Enough to bring a permanent change to his wayward heart? She was about to find out.

Nashville was a big place and would have been much more formidable if not for my father's family. They welcomed us with love and kindness. They understood him, and they appreciated Mom's love for him despite his erratic behavior.

Little did I know I would bond with his family for the rest of my life.

My father had arranged a first-floor apartment for us in a big old house with a long, wraparound front porch. The Southerners called it a veranda. The home was nestled among tall trees, with green grass all around. A high, wooden fence painted gray lined one side of the driveway, which gave us a secure feeling in such a big home. Inside, the ceilings were high and the rooms large. In the hallway, a grate lay over the furnace below. It looked to be a long way down when Mikey and I peered into it the first day.

Mom and my father Johnny had one bedroom. Mikey and I shared the other, with bunk beds. I slept on top since I was four and a half and could climb up.

My memories about Nashville are a little vague, though. I barely remember seeing my father while we were there. He was gone most of the time. Mom's fears were playing out in the old, familiar way. He hadn't changed at all. Not a lick.

But there are two things about Nashville I will always remember: The first is the stray kitten.

I was outside playing with my brother and playmates, who lived in other apartments in the old house, when the kitten wandered onto our porch. It was so little and hungry, gray and white, soft and cuddly. It purred and meowed as we all took turns holding it. Mom came to its rescue with a little milk in a big cereal bowl.

As it was lapping up the milk, with all of us children standing around like little saviors, we heard her coming. Mrs. Gray. The landlady.

Oh, but she could be stern. And, that day, she was downright mean.

"There will be no pets!" she screeched.

And with that, she grabbed the kitten by the scruff of its tiny neck and hurled it violently over the tall gray fence.

I ran sobbing to my mother, with blinding tears and a searing impression on my soul of what cruelty looks like.

The second thing I remember about Nashville: Candy, Mandy and Sandy, my beloved paper dolls, triplets with brown hair and big blue eyes. Bertie and Uncle Clarence sent them to me in a big box that also contained a toy for Mikey and food for all of us.

Mom carefully cut out three sets of matching outfits for my triplets: three plaid jackets and skirts, three snowsuits and muffs, and three cowgirl getups.

Each morning after breakfast, I headed to the living room and decided which outfit to dress them in—until the day I couldn't find them.

Mom helped me search high and low. They were nowhere in the apartment. Or so we thought.

Then Mom looked down the old grate in the hallway. Lying in a crumpled heap, far out of reach, were my beloved Candy, Mandy and Sandy, stuffed through the grate by my brother's own, little hands. I was inconsolable.

Although Mom, Bertie and Uncle Clarence tried to replace them, they could never find their equals. Candy, Mandy, and Sandy were gone.

Meanwhile, Mom was dealing with a much larger issue. Once again, she was about to lose her marriage—and possibly her children—as she recognized the truth about her husband.

Johnny could not change. Johnny was wayward.

She couldn't take the heartbreak any longer, and she couldn't make it work without his help. Once and for all, she gave up on him.

After months of trying, she loaded Mikey and me on the train for the ride back north to Pennsylvania—this time for good.

A New and
Lasting Home

After we got back from Nashville, Mom took Mikey to live with her in a boarding house. By day, he stayed with a babysitter while Mom worked. At night, she held him in her arms in the room they shared. It wasn't much, but at least it wasn't that crowded apartment on Railroad Street with the tormenting cousin.

Once again, Mom faced an uncertain future. The only thing she knew for sure now was that her marriage was over, really over. A hard worker, it didn't take Mom long to discover she was a good waitress. Customers enjoyed her red-lipstick smile and her kindheartedness. They left generous tips lying under their plates. That tip money paid for the room at the boarding house, the babysitter, and food. Mom began to feel that one day soon she could provide for her children. She could get them back together.

Meanwhile, I stayed at Bertie's house. And picked right up as though I'd never left. I played on the carpeted living-room floor with my toys and traveled the prairies with the ceramic stagecoach. While nothing could replace Candy, Mandy and Sandy, the stagecoach was still my favorite of Bertie's knickknacks.

Bertie and Uncle Clarence welcomed me back with open arms and more than a few tears.

My memory of my father faded into a deep place in my heart, as my new home became a secure anchor in my life. Bertie cooked hot meals every day, and sometimes my mom and Mikey joined us. As time went by, Bertie and Uncle Clarence's home became my home. Finally, Mom had to accept that I would live there. But at least she could keep her son.

Bertie had married Uncle Clarence when she was working at the local shirt factory. She was twenty; he was twenty-one. Her job at the factory allowed her to sit and practice the sewing skills her mother had taught her. At the time, Bertie had had no hope she would ever marry. As she often said, who would want her with a deformed body? Little did she know that a man with a big heart would enter her life and fall in love with her. It happened through a friend.

"Can I give you a lift home?" Bertie's tall, blonde girlfriend asked her one day after work. "My boyfriend just got a new car, and he's here to pick me up."

Bertie was glad to get a ride. That mile-long walk home was hard. She climbed into the backseat of the new, two-door car, and her vivacious girlfriend chatted away in the front. Bertie could never recall much of what she said, though. She was distracted by the driver glancing at her in his rearview mirror. All the way home, she caught him looking at her. She was self-conscious and thrilled at the same time. My, he was handsome.

When he pulled up at the curb in front of Bertie's rooming house, he held the seat forward so she could climb out. "I'll be seeing you," he said.

And he did. Uncle Clarence saw Bertie every day for the next seventy-two years.

When he first looked at Bertie, he saw her dark, flashing eyes. He was attracted. Soon after, he experienced her sharp wit and recognized her good heart. He never saw the deformed body.

Not long after they married, they made their home in a spacious apartment on Main Street in an early nineteenth-century building that had been stylish and impressive in its day. Two-thirds Georgian with Flemish bond brickwork, the home had been a centerpiece of residence and commerce. The Flemish bond was believed to provide aesthetic appeal and strength to the structure. This style of building, a variant of the Georgian style, was adapted for urban settings in Pennsylvania's early cities. Since they were both working, they could afford the rent in the well-maintained building that had seen better days.

The first floor of the 1830s building housed various forms of commerce over the years: a mercantile shop, dry goods and notions, and a fine china shop. Eventually, the first floor was divided into two sections, each housing separate businesses. Through my growing-up years, a stationery store and a state-run liquor store occupied the first floor. The former residence, in the past comprising the entire second floor, was remodeled into three apartments. The third floor was an attic.

Then there was the dusty, dirty cellar with the big, coal-fired furnace that served all the floors. To help with the rent, Uncle Clarence shoveled large buckets of coal into the belly of that furnace every winter. Early in the mornings, after work in the evenings, before bed and in the middle of the night, he fired that furnace. He never missed.

From the front of the building, they accessed their apartment through a door situated at ground level on Main Street, between the two stores. A steep staircase inside led to the second-floor apartments. At the back of their apartment, a fire escape led from an old tar roof to a dirt parking lot below. The flat, tar roof extended across the back of all three apartments on the second floor and was used as a walkway to get from one apartment to the other. Two apartments faced forward to Main Street; one faced back toward the dirt parking lot behind. Bertie's overlooked Main Street. Uncle Clarence built a screened-in back porch on the tar roof off the kitchen, which became the center of many family meals.

Bertie and Uncle Clarence's apartment was spacious and convenient, modest, and clean. But it also knew sadness. The sadness of losing a child. They had longed for children, so Bertie had become pregnant, praying she wouldn't have difficulties delivering because of her back. Their fears were realized when their infant child was laid to rest with a tiny headstone that read "Beloved Son." There were no more hopes for a child of their own.

Years went by with a lonely longing hovering in the air of their home. For a period of time, they took in Uncle Clarence's 13-year-old nephew, Jacque. They loved him like a son. Bertie always referred to him as "my Jacque." He stayed with them through college. When he graduated, he began teaching in Philadelphia and moved out, leaving their home empty once again.

Then they took me in.

Their joy in having a child in their home was complete. Almost.

My tall, farmer grandfather Pappy was worried. He worried about my mom, his youngest daughter, and whether she could keep things going. He worried about her children being separated. He wanted us raised together.

So he talked to Bertie about his worries and asked her to take in my brother Mikey also. "They belong together," he said.

Bertie was torn. She pitied my brother, but, with a crippled body at forty years of age, she didn't think she could raise more than one small child.

My grandfather, however, was persistent.

None of us knew, then, how Pappy eventually would get his way.

Divine
Intervention

Under the glow of the pink lamp in my new bedroom at Bertie's, she inspired my faith in God the first night she read to me from the Bible. The years eventually proved that God's hand would touch my life over and over. The first time I saw the hand of God, I was a little over five and enjoying my new life on Main Street with Bertie and Uncle Clarence. I missed my mother and two-and-a-half-year-old brother, but here I felt safe and protected.

Then the hand of God showed up one summer's day.

Mom and my brother came to Bertie's early that morning. It was a short walk from the rooming house. After breakfast for everyone, Bertie and Mom set up Pappy's old wringer washer on the back porch to wash the clothes. It would be a long day for them, as each clean piece of laundry had to be hung on the clothesline they had stretched over the old tar roof.

So we wouldn't be in their way, Mom and Bertie arranged for Mikey and me to go to the public playground with Peetie, who watched us sometimes.

That day, Peetie was dressed in a white summer blouse and a striped, green-silk skirt with a crinoline petticoat. A little dressy for a playground, but an outfit I'll never forget.

Off we went, with Peetie holding Mikey's hand as Bertie and Mom dove into their pile of clothes, up to their elbows in sudsy water.

The playground had a large, round concrete swimming pool with the same three-foot depth all around for the safety of the children, who played here while their parents were working.

There were also a small, covered pavilion for doing crafts; a swing set; monkey bars; and a sliding board with eleven steep steps. The slide was mounted on a crooked concrete slab, and one corner of the slab jutted out three inches.

Mikey was fearless. He climbed the sliding board before anyone noticed. Peetie had her back turned, talking to a friend. I was watching other kids.

Then Mikey called my name from the top step, the tippy top of that tall sliding board.

"Look at me, Bonnie! Watch me slide!" He flashed a baby-toothed grin. That was the last time he smiled for weeks.

He slipped and tumbled all the way down the eleven stairs on the back of the slide—onto the concrete slab. That nasty corner ripped his forehead wide open, with a gaping gash nearly two inches long. Thick, red blood was gushing out.

With horror, Peetie picked him up, and we three ran like the wind. Peetie was crying. I was crying. Mikey wasn't crying.

He lay deadly still in Peetie's arms, just gushing blood.

We ran and ran and ran. The whole five blocks to Bertie's house. Peetie's white blouse and green-striped skirt were drenched in blood.

As we rounded the corner to the dirt parking lot in back, Mom and Bertie spotted us from the porch above.

Mom came screaming down the fire escape and met us halfway in the parking lot. She scooped her bleeding son into her arms. "My baby! My baby!" Tears soaked her face at the horrible sight. Her baby's forehead gashed. His little T-shirt soaked in blood.

Bertie had called the doctor down the street to alert him that an injured child was on the way. Mom ran down Main Street with Mikey in her arms, dodged cars as she crossed the busy highway, and kept running to the white house, to Doc Freeman. Her khaki capris and white summer blouse were now drenched in her child's blood.

A nurse was waiting with the door open at the top of the stairs. For several hours, the doctor and nurse worked to save my brother's life.

Much later that day, Mom carried him back to Bertie's and lay him on a bed in the spare bedroom, the one Jacque had recently vacated. It was as if the room had been prepared for this little boy, with its Hardy Boy mysteries in the bookcase and masculine overtones.

Mikey was unmoving, unconscious, and gravely ill.

The doctor had wrapped a turban of gauze around Mikey's entire head. We could barely see his eyes, not that it mattered. His eyes were closed and stayed that way for many days. His condition was critical. This little warrior had a long road ahead.

The days stretched on. Mikey still lay unresponsive. Bertie and Mom took turns providing around-the-clock nursing care.

Mikey slowly woke up, then lay more days in a doll-like state. Eyes open, but no recognition.

Finally, he began to rally, and we were overjoyed. He was going to live and be whole again. Thank God!

And then one day, he was well enough to come to the dinner table. It was there that our lives took a dramatic turn. It was there that the hand of God perfected the work begun that summer's day of the accident.

The Unbreakable Bond

Weary and exhausted from long hours on her feet, still at work, Mom received a phone call from Bertie with the exciting news that Mikey was rallying and about to have supper. It wouldn't be long until she could hold him all night in her arms again at their rooming house. What Mom didn't know was that, once again, she was going to be asked to survive on her own.

For the first time since his accident, Mikey was able to come to the table for dinner. He was still wearing his gauze turban but was almost back to normal. And he had developed a healthy appetite.

Uncle Clarence placed a red step stool from the pantry close to the wall at the back of the kitchen table. With its high back, it made a perfect child's chair. For safety, he tied Mikey in with an old necktie. He fiddled and fussed with the necktie for the longest time, wanting to be sure it was secure. Then he pulled the stool and Mikey close to him.

Bertie was just finishing the meal at the stove, and she set the dish of hot, buttered mashed potatoes on the table. Without hesitation, Mikey dove his fingers into the dish and pulled out a fistful of gooey mashed potatoes.

Something came over Uncle Clarence as he watched the small boy suck on his fistful of potatoes. He became overwhelmed with love. Maybe he saw an image of his own son, who had died at birth. Maybe he remembered the many times Mikey had gone to bed hungry.

With a father's gentle hand, Uncle Clarence shook the mashed potatoes from Mikey's fist and said, "It's OK, son. You can put these down. We'll put them on a plate for you. You'll never go hungry again. You'll stay here and live with us."

With these words, Bertie knew she had taken a son to raise, too.

From that day on, the bond was set between Uncle Clarence, who needed a son, and Mikey, who needed a father.

So, my brother and I were raised together in that apartment on Main Street with Bertie and Uncle Clarence. By Divine order. Pappy's prayers and pleas had been answered.

But something precious was missing. Our mother would not join us. She was left alone at the rooming house.

I Hurt

Mikey, now nearly three years old, was an active little boy who loved the outdoors. Although the scar on his forehead from the terrible accident on the playground would last his entire life, the wound was healed. He was getting comfortable in his new home with Bertie and Uncle Clarence.

Since there was no backyard in which to play, Mikey entertained himself for hours outside on the flat tar roof that connected the three apartments in our building.

Bertie kept a watchful eye on him from the kitchen window.

He didn't need a lot of playthings except for his toy soldiers and tricycle. That tricycle took him dangerously close to the edge of the roof, some fourteen feet above the ground.

No matter how many times Bertie told him not to go to the edge, his sense of adventure drew him back to the dangerous precipice again and again. Just like when he was on the sliding board at the playground six months earlier, Mikey was fearless.

Bertie gave him freedom to play in his own way. She worried, though, the entire time he rode his tricycle. When he parked it and attended to his soldiers, she was always relieved. Knowing that his imagination would keep him occupied with his little plastic men for a long while, she could safely return to her cooking. But Bertie observed something that broke her heart as she watched him from the window. It had to do with the normal scrapes and bruises of children at play.

When Mikey hurt himself while playing, he didn't come into the house seeking comfort from Bertie. Instead, he stood against the wall of the apartment building with his back turned to the window and his arms folded over his chest. Rocking back and forth, he endured his pain alone.

Bertie would rush to him when she saw that he was hurt. She usually found him crying softly with no indication that he expected to be comforted. This happened several times.

Mikey had learned at a tender age that he had to face his hurts by himself.

This imprint was stamped on his heart by the necessity of Mom's long work hours while living on Railroad Street. As much as she would have wanted to, she could not be there to comfort her small son. When I left, too, to stay with Bertie and Uncle Clarence, Mikey was *really* alone. Totally defenseless at such a young age, he had no one to comfort him from his older cousin's bullying while Mom was away at work.

It stands to reason when he first came to live at Bertie's, he was his own little army of one.

Grade School Years

Life Savers

By the time I started first grade, Mikey and I were well-adjusted to our home with Bertie and Uncle Clarence. Through sheer determination and hard work, Mom had saved enough money to move into the back apartment next to Bertie's. Now she was just across the tar roof. She had longed to be close to her children, and we had missed her. Living this close, she could be in our lives much more. We were overjoyed.

I wasn't quite six years old when I started first grade in the old elementary school with the creaky wooden floors. My, how those floors took to a shine. Kindly janitors, their big buckets filled with pleasant-smelling water and wax, faithfully polished those floors until they gleamed.

Elderly Miss Kline was my teacher. She was kind but strict. She wore her white hair in a bun, with some wispy strands that fell across her marshmallow-soft cheeks. She liked to read to us from her chair in front of the class. Most days, I loved to hear her soothing voice as she read the stories.

But there was one day when I didn't even hear the words she read. I was distracted by a broken heart.

Mom was gone a lot working her waitress shifts at a restaurant—some days from mid-morning to early evening, other days from early evening to late at night. On mornings when she wasn't at work, she came across the roof to Bertie's kitchen to have coffee and a bite to eat with us. Bertie always made sure I had a good breakfast before I left for school.

When Mom joined us on those mornings, she brought her tip money from the day before. Bertie was good at math and loved figuring amounts. She enjoyed counting Mom's tip money for her while I ate my toast and drank my milk. Mom was beginning to get on her feet and starting to enjoy life again. My father was now a fading memory in all our lives. We never heard from him.

One morning, Mom brought me a surprise of Butter Rum Life Savers. She knew I loved them. So off I went to school with my prized gift from my mother in my pocket.

When I got to school, I neatly placed my books on top of my desk, just like Miss Kline always asked us to do. Miss Kline liked things done in a certain way.

That day, I also lay my treasure, the Butter Rum Life Savers, on top of my desk.

As Miss Kline began to read from the front of the room, I popped a Life Saver into my mouth and started to settle in for a good story. Until.

Until she looked up and saw me with the Life Savers. Miss Kline liked things done in a certain way, and I was about to learn that she didn't like us eating in class.

She stopped reading and demanded that I throw my Life Savers into the trash can.

I hesitated, a brief moment. She gave me a look that said she meant business, so I walked to the front of the classroom and threw my Life Savers in the trash can—feeling as if I were throwing away a piece of my mother.

It's hard to explain how a simple pack of Life Savers could mean so much. But it did. I didn't get to see my mother as much as I wanted. Our lives were joined, but separate. She worked long hours to pay her rent and help raise Mikey and me. We were bonded through her unconditional and forever love for us. When she presented me with a gift, I always treasured it.

Those Life Savers were an emotional connection to my mom. And I had lost them.

I returned to my seat, and sat there heartbroken. I didn't hear a word of the story after that.

There was only one thing to do. I had to get my Life Savers back.

My good friend in first grade was Rosalie, who sat next to me. Good-natured Rosalie, with her red hair and gentle ways. Tall for her age, like me.

While Miss Kline read the story, with her eyes down and concentrating, I whispered to Rosalie, asking her to tiptoe over to the trash can and retrieve my Life Savers.

She didn't want to. But I kept pleading.

Finally, off she went, tiptoeing, then pretending to throw away a tissue.

She tiptoed back, sat down quietly, and lay the Life Savers on my desk.

That's when I froze. What if Miss Kline saw me? What if I got caught, again?

Just then, Miss Kline looked straight at me—and at my Life Savers.

She firmly questioned how I got them back. I told her Rosalie got them out of the trash. Rosalie gasped, looked at me but said nothing.

Miss Kline scolded both of us. Only one of us deserved it.

That day, I learned I was corruptible. When push came to shove, I caved. I persuaded Rosalie to do something she knew was wrong. Then I lied to protect myself. I had betrayed my friend.

I lost my Life Savers, again. And much more.

Faded Dress

My shame in second grade started with the blue dress with white polka dots. How I loved it when I saw it hanging in the five and dime that summer right before school started. I had to have it.

Then, no matter how many times it was washed, I loved it more and more. With each washing, it got softer and softer. With each washing, it became more and more faded.

I didn't notice. I loved that dress.

But there came a day when I was embarrassed by it. It was the day I first discovered the feeling of shame. A feeling that takes you to a low place. A deep, dark, small place.

It was a beautiful spring day. The tulips were in full bloom in shades of yellow, red, and orange. Yellow daffodils turned their heads toward heaven for long kisses of sunshine. The cold and snowy Pennsylvania winter was behind us, and everyone's heart was a little lighter.

Our teacher, Miss Dorman, obviously loved spring. She had arranged a special event on that fair day for all the girls in class and our mothers. She called it a "Mother-Daughter Tea."

Somehow, I had lost that invitation and forgotten all about the party. I was surprised when I returned from lunch to see the classroom all decked out in pretty little cups and saucers, fancy cookies, and an assortment of teas. Miss Dorman had put on her Sunday dress and wore pearls around her neck. She looked elegant.

When my classmates began arriving back from lunch, I noticed that they, too, were dressed in their finest pretty dresses and good Sunday shoes.

With each girl who came into the classroom, my heart sank deeper and deeper into burning embarrassment. Tears hung dangerously close as I realized there was a party, and I wasn't dressed for it. Then the twins came in. Now my heart really sank.

Chrissy and Ann were my best friends. Chrissy with her short, curly brown hair. Ann with her long brown hair, streaked with gold. They were popular and pretty, and they were dressed for the party. Their white chiffon dresses billowed with yards and yards of crinoline petticoats underneath. Ann's dress had a pale pink sash; Chrissy's sash was pale blue. Lacy white anklets with patent-leather white Sunday shoes completed their splendid outfits.

As they sat on each side of me, in chairs pulled into a semicircle for the tea, I became overcome with shame. My faded blue dress was pathetic. How could I have forgotten such an important event?

Chrissy and Ann's big dresses spilled over my lap on both sides and completely covered my faded dress. I kept batting them down in a desperate attempt to matter. The twins kept repositioning their crinolines to keep their dresses from wrinkling.

I felt small, insignificant, and hopeless.

Just when I thought I could feel no lower, the mothers came into our classroom. All tastefully dressed, especially Chrissy and Ann's mother. She was lovely and stood out.

Neither my mother nor my aunt could have come even if I had remembered the party. They had to work. Mom was working at the restaurant and Bertie, to help support my brother and me, had gone to work at the local five and dime store.

Despite that, at least I could have put on one of my better dresses. My faded blue dress, which I had so loved, was now the object of my shame.

I met shame that day. It changed me, and I carried it deep inside. Until the day when I no longer allowed shame to have a place in my heart.

Our New Dad

My brother and I grew up thinking we were rich. At Bertie's, our home was warm on cold winter nights, hot food was in the oven, and affirming love was all around us. We were enveloped in riches.

By now, Mikey and I had come to think of Uncle Clarence as Dad. It began with Mikey sitting on his lap one evening when he was about three years old and asking him, "Are you my uncle or my daddy?" Dad responded, "I'm a little of both, Son." To which Mikey joyfully proclaimed, "Then I'm going to call you Uncle Daddy!" Uncle Daddy eventually evolved to just Dad. Uncle Clarence was in every sense our dad.

Dad's hands and feet were never idle.

After long days at the furniture factory, Dad came home dirty and smelling like sawdust, with a number two pencil still wedged behind his ear. Dad was smart with numbers. He had graduated from a two-year business school and could have made a career working with numbers had it not been for his first love: making things out of wood.

In a woodworking shop he set up in the attic, he produced his creations. His custom cabinetry and hand-crafted staircases graced some of the fine homes in town.

Plus, he kept the coal-fired furnace going in our apartment building at all hours of the day and night. The extra money was spent wisely on food, shelter, clothing, and special Christmas mornings.

That was in addition to driving the main engine for the Cumberland Valley Hose Company, where he served as president. When the fire alarm sounded, Dad dropped anything he was doing and ran with all his might across the street to the fire house. By the time the other volunteers arrived, Dad had the fire engine outside and ready to rush to the fire.

No, Dad's hands and feet were never idle.

But without a doubt, Dad's most loving work played out at the back of our apartment building in a place we called "Down Back." Here his work was more than professional; it was personal.

Down Back was just a rut-filled, dirt parking lot at the rear of our apartment building. Shoppers parked in this dusty lot to access the businesses in the front of our building. After parking, they headed for Main Street through an archway that separated our building from Miss Nancy's home. No rippling waves of green grass between our toes or pleasing daffodils in the spring, Down Back was a simple place where Mikey and I played. Dad made it our paradise.

Down Back extended to the far corner of our building and included an abandoned room that had been empty since the late 1800s. It had been used for storage by the various merchants who established businesses on the first floor of our building. A couple of years after Dad and Bertie took me and Mikey in, Dad asked the landlord for permission to build us a playhouse in the small room. Gratefully, permission was granted.

Dad cleared the cobwebs and sorted through the remnants of the storage room's former life: discarded crates, odd pieces of lumber, and broken chairs.

Inside the storage room and behind a closed door was a set of steps that led upstairs to a former wing of the family residence, now Mom's apartment. The door at the top of those old stairs had been boarded up.

As the steps now served no purpose, Dad locked the door so we wouldn't be tempted to climb and fall.

Despite the dusty, dirty little room, Dad had a vision. For weeks, he worked evenings, all day Saturdays, and Sundays after church. He transformed the room into a playhouse that would capture our imaginations.

He painted the outside of the door white, but inside left it in its rugged, unpainted state. The rustic look of the unpainted door lent a homey feel to the room. He covered the dilapidated walls in white sheetrock with perfectly ordered nails, and set a new, lower ceiling to give a cozy feeling inside. He built and painted shelves on the walls on both sides, and laid a frayed red carpet over a new planked floor to provide a feeling of warmth.

He gave our playhouse, the tiny room, an imaginary dividing line down the middle, between my space and my brother's. Mikey's shelf was covered with a scattering of trucks and balls. Mine held Baby Susan and Pee Baby, my two dolls, and my pink-and-black play dishes.

The room wasn't heated—that would have been too costly—but on very cold days we plugged in a small space heater, and the multi-paned window on Mikey's side let in warm sunshine and a lot of light.

In our completed playhouse, Mikey and I got lost for hours in our own worlds of make-believe. On the red carpet, he drove his trucks for miles, all the while talking out loud as he took first one driver's part, then the other's.

On my side, I served up home-cooked dinners on my fancy plastic dishes. Pee Baby got her bottle filled with real water and, true to her name, promptly needed to be changed. There was much for a busy mommy and a trucker to do.

Next, Dad created a playground for us outside the playhouse.

First, he scoured the scrap yards to come up with the materials for a swing set. The metal posts, which he grounded in a bed of cement, were rusted and chipped, four inches in diameter, sturdy and sure. Those posts weren't going anywhere, which is exactly what Dad planned. Then he bolted two sets of heavy chains to the top of each post to securely hold the thick, wooden seats.

Dad had a way of knowing that, when it came to swinging, youngsters want to soar. And soar we did, high above the top of the playhouse door and almost touching the windows of Mom's apartment, which was just above on the second floor. Never once did those posts even hint at leaving the ground.

Then he built us a seesaw, a long, thick wooden board balanced on a wood fulcrum. Dad sanded the board until it was smooth as silk. Big, shiny metal bolts held it firmly in place. Mikey and I rocked back and forth to our hearts' content on long summer days.

Finally, Dad built us a sandbox across the lot from our playhouse. Situated in the corner at the back fire escape, it was framed by Miss Nancy's garden wall. It was perfectly shaped out of wood, four feet deep and five feet wide.

Dad filled it with eight inches of moist, soft sand.

Shaded by Miss Nancy's massive tulip poplar tree, Mikey and I played for hours with our buckets and shovels. Despite all the shoppers coming and going, none of our toys was ever stolen.

Just outside the sandbox was my flower garden, surrounding a telephone pole. Every year when the warmer weather arrived in late April, Bertie stopped at the Pague and Fegan Hardware Store and purchased a couple of seed packages of bright yellow marigolds. Year after year, Bertie and I faithfully planted those seeds, fully anticipating seeing their golden glory in June.

Sure enough, every summer they sprang to life, vivacious and captivating, in that sandy soil surrounding the telephone pole. I couldn't bear to pick something so beautiful. I was content just to look at them every summer day.

We not only enjoyed this playground ourselves, we invited friends to play there. I loved it when my best friend Jerry, from just up the street, came to play on the seesaw with me. Other neighborhood kids came, too, and rode high on our swings.

Life was abundant there in that old dirt parking lot, in our private paradise that Dad built with his own hands, his ingenuity, and a father's love—which transcended biology and blood.

Mikey and I were, indeed, rich.

This Thing Called Love

Donny was a dreamboat and my first crush. That blond hair. Those big white teeth. That slow, easy walk. I felt fortunate that this eight-year-old heartbreaker ended up in my third-grade class. And he was coming to my birthday party.

Every year like clockwork, I turned a year older on October 30. This year I was going to be eight and, on the Saturday closest to my birthday, Mom and Bertie threw me a birthday bash. They prepared orange chiffon cake a mile high, perched on a beautiful glass pedestal, ham sandwiches, and potato salad, plus party hats, streamers, and games.

My invitation list consisted of Chrissy and Ann, my best friends; Jerry, my other best friend from just up the street; my brother; my cousin Jackie; and a few classmates. And, of course, Donny.

We cleaned the house until it sparkled. I had my usual chores of dusting and polishing the furniture and hanging up my clothes from their familiar landing spot on top of the hamper in the bathroom.

Finally, the day of the party arrived. The house was spit-shined, the tall cake was majestic on its perch, and good aromas were coming from the kitchen. When the doorbell rang, I answered it with anticipation and a new dress. One by one, they all arrived. Every last one of them.

After we finished eating the cake, it was time to play games. I most remember spin the bottle.

We kids sat in a circle on the floor in the living room. Bertie and Mom watched over us. As the bottle spun this direction and that, my heart pounded. Perhaps Donny would spin, and it would point to me.

He did, and it did. He had to kiss me.

He kissed me shyly, and quickly, on the cheek.

On the spur of the moment, Mom ran for her camera in the next room. When she returned, I was about to take my turn spinning the bottle, but she said, "Hold up." Then she asked Donny to kiss me again so she could get a picture.

His cheeks blushing, he kissed me again. Just as quickly, and in the same spot as before.

Mom's camera failed to snap. "Could you do that one more time?" she asked.

A third time, now embarrassed, Donny kissed my cheek again, and Mom got the shot she wanted.

Someone might have thought it was a conspiracy. It wasn't. But try telling that to the twins.

The following Monday, still feeling Donny's sweet kisses on my cheek, I went off to school with a bounce in my step.

Standing guard at the classroom door were the twins, madder than wet hens. Everyone had to pass through their defensive stance.

Then I arrived.

"We know what your mother was doing at your party," Ann, looking beautiful even when angry, declared in an icy tone with her hands on her hips. "She was just making Donny kiss you over and over. Well, he doesn't love *you*. He loves Chrissy."

Chrissy, meanwhile, just stared at me. She didn't have a word to say. Her twin had said it all.

Chrissy, with her short brown curly hair and big blue eyes, was a doll. And now I learned that Donny loved her, not me. My heart sank. My bounce bounced away.

I slithered to my desk, not at all sure about this thing called love.

But my heart continued to have a softness for Donny. Weeks turned into months, and I continued to dream about him. He didn't notice me, but I didn't let that deter me.

On Valentine's Day, I dreamed about Donny in my real heart as I worked away on my paper heart in art class. I needed to make it extra special. It was large and perfectly shaped, and I wrote in big letters on the front, "To Donny. Love, Bonnie." I folded it in half and handed it to my designated messenger, good old Rosalie. She still blessed me by being my friend even after my cowardly betrayal in first grade.

Sweet Rosalie walked my heart right over to Donny. He was sitting at a table with a few boys, all working on their art projects. I watched from the other side of the room as he read my inscription.

Without looking up, he ripped my heart into pieces. Then he quietly got up from the table, walked his slow, easy walk to the trash can, and threw away my heart.

With my paper heart trashed, I got over love. I got over Donny.

Happily, my third-grade teacher, Marilyn Burkholder, taught me about a different kind of love: a teacher's love and kindness for all those she touched. I might have lost Donny, but I gained so much more from the beautiful and elegant Mrs. Burkholder.

Bright orange lipstick, warm brown eyes with hints of amber, a creamy complexion, and raven black hair—that was Mrs. Burkholder. I thought she was one of the prettiest women I had ever seen.

Mrs. Burkholder did not have to work. She had grown up in her father's mansion on the other end of Main Street. Manicured gardens, luxury cars, and a grand staircase were all part of her upbringing. Her father was the President of Peerless Furniture and they had one of the biggest factories in the region. He was my dad's big boss. In fact, Dad had helped build that staircase on one of his many moonlighting projects.

Even more than her outer beauty, Mrs. Burkholder was known for her inner beauty. She was kind, soft-spoken, and full of grace—everything I wanted to be.

She took an instant liking to me. Maybe it was whom I knew: Dad. She was always kind to him when greeting him on the street or in a store. Perhaps she had watched him build that staircase and appreciated his strong work ethic.

I couldn't have known then how life would turn out for this kind and lovely teacher. One day many years later, I read in the newspaper about her tragic horseback-riding accident. All that beauty, grace, and goodness, gone from this world.

But she had touched my life forever in a remarkable way by showing kindness to me and her other students.

By the end of the third grade, I had learned there were different types of love other than the way Mom, Bertie, and Dad loved me. Even though some love doesn't turn out the way we want, love is good.

Bad Words

When I was in elementary school, it was safe for a younger child to walk alone to school. I took my time on my solitary, daily journey to grade school, jumping on all the cellar doors along the way and running up and down the steps of homes as I meandered along.

After school, I would stop at Jensen's store and spend my nickel on penny candy. A small brown sack would be filled almost to the brim with red hot dollars, Mary Janes, and chocolate malted milk balls. I'd eat every bite before I hit the town square several blocks away.

One morning on my way to school, I heard some "big boys," probably in junior high, using a new word as they passed by me. They used it at least three times. It was a word I had never heard before. Because of what would happen later, I even remember which house I was in front of when I heard the new word.

I couldn't wait to try it.

My opportunity came that evening as Bertie, Dad, Mikey and I were all gathered around the black and white television set in the living room. I was stretched out on the couch, Dad was in his favorite easy chair, Bertie was in hers, and Mikey was lying on the floor in front of the TV. A favorite program had just concluded and a new one was about to start.

Coming on next was Arthur Godfrey's Talent Scouts. On the show, unrecognized talented people, discovered by Godfrey's "talent scouts," would audition and perform their acts with the hopes of stardom in their hearts. The winner was determined by audience applause which was measured by a meter.

Bertie and Dad loved it, Mikey tolerated it, and I loathed it. It seemed so slow and drawn out. I always felt a let-down when Arthur came on the television.

So, as I lay there on the couch, I remarked to no one in particular but loud enough for everyone in the room to hear me, "Oh, don't tell me that (expletive deleted) is coming on again."

Dad raised forward in his chair while Bertie put down her crochet hook. They both just stared at me when Dad finally said in a concerned tone, "What did you say?"

I repeated the word I had said. Only this time it had a question mark at the end.

After hearing what he thought he had heard, Dad said in a fatherly but stern voice, "Don't you ever use that term again. That is a bad word."

That's when I broke into tears and explained I had heard it from big boys on their way to school that morning.

I felt like a criminal. I didn't know that I had just passed from the age of innocence. All I did know was that I felt terrible. Like I let my parents down. Like I had done something awful.

What would have happened if Dad had not been there to guide me? How accustomed to that term might I have become? How might that have molded me in a direction quite different from the one I took in my life? Words are a part of who we are, how we think, and what we do. Words are a part of how others view us.

Profanity is the lazy way of talking. There are so many magnificent words in the English language to deploy into every sentence we speak. Why settle for vulgar terms that provide no depth of expression or richness of thought? Why settle for vulgarity when it adds no value, elegance, or respect for the speaker?

As for Arthur, he did quite well without my endorsement and my failed attempt to discredit him.

Rachel

Legend has it that she carried a switchblade and knew how to use it. She was described as mean and looking for a fight.

When I was around seven years old and on my way home from elementary school one day, someone pointed her out to me. But only after she passed by.

"That's Rachel," my classmate whispered.

Now I had a face to go with the reputation. She had short hair, piercing eyes, and a stocky body. From that day on, the sight of Rachel terrified me. I was convinced she was out to kill me.

Thus began my worrying ways, which lasted almost a lifetime.

Oh, I worried plenty about Rachel. At night, I would beg my mother to tell me Rachel had left town and could no longer harm me. Mom would hold me and say soothing things until I fell into a tormented sleep. But in the morning, the sick thud would hit my stomach as soon I opened my eyes. Rachel.

I didn't stop at just Rachel with my worrying ways. I worried that the house would burn down, that my family would die, that I would be left alone. Once worry gets a foothold, a lot of worry's cousins move in.

Then one day when I was eight years old, I really had something to worry about.

My cousin Jackie and I were standing in a small crowd at the town square waiting for the freight train to pass. Jackie was nine months older than me and a couple inches shorter. Her mom was my mom's twin sister. Just as Mom and her twin, my Aunt Bootie, were close, Jackie and I were close. Clad in our crisply starched Brownie outfits, we were on our way to the fire station a few blocks away. It was Memorial Day, and our Brownie troop was marching in the annual parade, which always formed at the firehouse.

The day was beautiful, with mild temperatures and clear blue skies. It was a pleasant relief from the long winter. That morning, the firemen had churned the homemade Grape-Nuts ice cream, always a crowd pleaser with its malty, crunchy flavor.

Up and down Main Street, people had placed lawn chairs on the sidewalk to get a good view of the parade. Marching bands from our town and neighboring communities were gathering into formation, decked out in their snappy uniforms, white gloves, and plumed hats. Beauty queens in long gowns and opera-length gloves were taking their seats on the flowery floats for the long, slow ride through town. Street vendors were lined up all along Main Street, selling hot dogs, french fries, soft pretzels, cotton candy, and icy, cold soft drinks.

Jackie and I loved cotton candy. As we waited for the freight train to pass, we watched the street vendor on the other side of the square twirling sugary strands into a delectable mound of pink, culinary delight. The longer we stood there, the more our mouths watered.

She was upon us before I had time to brace myself. When I saw her, my heart raced with fear. Rachel.

She came up behind us and silently maneuvered through the small crowd that was waiting for the train to pass. She stepped off the curb and edged close to the tracks. I watched her skirt blow around from the heft of the mighty locomotive that passed dangerously close to her. She wasn't afraid of anything. Undaunted and gutsy, she stood there watching each railroad car go by. Every now and then, she glanced back over her shoulder at the crowd. It was as if she was afraid someone was talking about her.

Jackie noticed her, but she still had her eye on the cotton candy across the street. Finally, she couldn't resist the pink, fluffy concoction any longer. She stood on her tiptoes, cupped her hand and whispered in my ear, "Let's go get some cotton candy."

Just then, Rachel whirled around and moved swiftly toward us. "Are you talking about me?" she demanded.

"No," I said lamely.

"No," Jackie said meekly.

"I'll smash your faces if you are," she said with a viciousness that left little doubt she meant it.

She stared us down for a few more seconds, which seemed like an eternity, then returned to her position close to the tracks. As we waited, I thought my heart would jump out of my chest. Finally, the last hulking train car passed, and she disappeared into the crowd of parade-goers.

That day, there would be no crossing the street for cotton candy. All I could do was turn around and run back home as fast as my unsteady legs would take me, little Jackie in tow. Tears gushing, we threw open the apartment door to the startled faces of Bertie and Dad. I spurted out in broken sentences what had happened. Jackie cried, too, as she tried to fill in the words I couldn't get out.

Bertie and Dad helped us dry our tears. Then, because our Brownie troop was marching in the parade, Dad gently said, "Come on, girls. I'll drive you to the parade."

"No," I protested. "A thousand times no." I was not going back out on that street.

But Dad insisted, and we finally gave in.

The streets were clogged. The alleyways were clogged. Parade-goers were everywhere, laughing merrily on the beautiful day. I envied their lightheartedness. I could see only dark days ahead. Rachel had just threatened me. Suddenly, everything had changed.

With patience and resolve, Dad weaved and cajoled his car through the crowded alleys to the Brownies' starting point at the firehouse. He was quiet as we pulled to the curb but said, "You girls have a good time. Everything is all right." I noticed that he swallowed hard.

Jackie and I joined our Brownie troop, which was already in formation. We marched, and I scanned. With every step, I eyed every street and every side street for that one, terrifying face.

I didn't see Rachel anymore that day.

But it didn't matter. I was marred for life.

My worrying began in earnest that lovely Memorial Day. I feared for my life. I hid from reality. I stayed home. I worried. I would only go out on the streets if someone went with me. Even then, my nerves were on edge and my stomach in knots, as I scanned for that solitary figure who had put the awful fear in me.

When I heard the lonely sound of a train whistle at night, I would say a prayer that Rachel was on that train and headed out of town. It was several years before Mom took me aside and told me the news that a coworker had shared with her: Rachel *had* moved out of town. Then she added, "She's gone for good and won't be coming back."

Whether that part about being gone for good was true or not, Mom had felt the need to say it. She would have done almost anything to release me from my self-imposed prison, which had destroyed my happiness and security.

That night, I slept soundly and deeply. The news of Rachel's leaving liberated me from the clutching shackles that had controlled my life. I was free—because Rachel was gone.

Rachel was a bully and a tough cookie. Her brazen personality had provoked the stories. But the more my fears grew, the more evil she became to me. The more my fears grew, the more power I gave her over me.

And thus I set in motion a cycle of fear and worry that accompanied me most of my life.

Years later, I learned that Rachel had *not* moved away as Mom was told. She continued to make her home right there in my hometown. When I had been in my twenties, Rachel had passed away.

One day, I dug deep inside and confronted my feelings about Rachel. The old fears surfaced. It hurt to remember, but the feelings lost their charge over me as I practiced feeling unconditionally fearless. As with any bully, Rachel only had the power I gave her. I took my power back. That's when I knew real freedom and found lasting joy.

Sometimes when I hear the lonely whistle of a distant train late at night, I think of Rachel. May she rest in peace.

Moneyed School

"Camay makes me smooth. It keeps me pretty, too. I use Camay every day. How about you?" So went the lines of my part in Mrs. Baer's fourth-grade play.

It wasn't Mrs. Baer who selected me for the part, but one of her student teachers, Miss Norman, who was as kind as she was pretty.

When she spoke with me during milk break one day and asked me to play the role, a warm feeling surged through me. She wanted *me* to play someone pretty. It gave me reason to float on air. After all, Donny had ripped my Valentine to shreds. *He* didn't think I was pretty. But the student teacher did. My heart soared for weeks.

I was in a new school. Bertie, Mom, and Dad had taken me away from my former classmates and plopped me into Mrs. Baer's class at the upper end of town.

My brother was the reason. Mikey was starting first grade at this school and everyone thought it was a good idea for me to be there with him, so I could look out for him and he wouldn't be alone in the new place. In the end, we both ended up being alone, except that we were alone together.

My previous school had been made up of regular kids whose parents were mostly working-class. My new school was filled with middle- and upper-class kids whose parents were doctors, teachers, and business owners. They were smart, well-dressed, and well-mannered.

I felt completely out of place.

Thank goodness for Kathy, my best and only friend in fourth grade. She lived in a small house on an ordinary street nearby and seemed more like a regular kid. Kathy and I talked all the time.

Mrs. Baer had every reason to be annoyed with our endless chatter back and forth across the aisle. We talked even more when one of Mrs. Baer's student teachers was in front of the class.

One day in total frustration, a student teacher, Mr. Lime, asked the class what he should do about our nonstop talking. A fellow classmate swiftly raised his hand and righteously announced that we should be made to put our heads down on our desks. As I sat there with my head resting on my folded arms, I thought how silly and annoying Kathy and I must have seemed to our classmate who so willingly suggested this mild punishment.

Fourth grade was a just a blip, but rubbing elbows with the smart, moneyed kids in town served a purpose. I learned about income differences and how those differences can show up in manners, grades, and expectations. A few years later, my need to fit in with these kids would leave a hollow feeling in my memory of trying to be something I'm not.

The Beating

When he started school, Mikey's vivid imagination and love of adventure could cause him to lose focus on his lessons and get into mischief. He was a little jokester and sometimes misbehaved in class. It led to the worst beating of his life.

The beating happened one day in school, about the second grade. As in all the times before when Mikey got hurt, he didn't say anything to Bertie and Dad about it.

That evening, Bertie went to his room to call him for dinner and found him lying on his bed. His arms were folded under his head, and he was staring at the ceiling. He was still dressed in his corduroy school trousers. Normally, he would rush home from school, change his clothes, and go outside to play until supper time. That night, he didn't want any supper. He was solemn and quiet.

Bertie and Dad knew something was wrong.

At bath time, Bertie saw the signs of trauma on Mikey's buttocks and thighs. They were red and swollen and turning black, purple, and blue from what appeared to be a vicious beating. After they questioned him, he told them it was delivered by the elementary school principal. He had used a wooden paddle. Evidently, Mikey had acted out or not paid attention once too often.

Bertie cried and called Mom at work to tell her what had happened. Dad was deeply hurt and angry.

Bertie and Dad disciplined my brother and me when we deserved it. They sent us to our rooms or withheld our allowance when we acted inappropriately. They recognized that children need to understand boundaries. They taught us right from wrong, but never raised a hand to us in anger.

There was no stopping Dad's response to what he considered an unusually severe punishment. Taking time away from work the next day, Dad paid a visit to the principal. Separated by a counter which provided a protective barrier for the principal's office, Dad looked him in the eye and threatened him with a similar beating if he ever hurt his "boy" again. Dad grew up rough-and-tumble. He meant what he said.

The consequential bruises showed the beating was delivered by a hand of rage. Bertie and Dad could not reconcile how a second grader deserved such a show of force. This type of beating was not meant merely as discipline. This type of beating was intended to settle a score. The score of someone's outsized ego that suffered an offense from a seven-year-old boy.

Time would prove that my brother would always bear his pain alone.

Summer

At first, I heard the quiet. Was anyone else at home? I was struggling to wake up. It was a summer morning and, as usual, I was sleeping late.

As my eyes blinked open, I heard the sounds of Main Street drifting through my open bedroom window. It was a friendly sound of shoppers, farmers, and neighbors greeting one another. It was summer. Summer in a small town. Summer on Main Street.

For most of June and all of July and August until Labor Day, my brother Mikey and I slept late every morning. His bedroom was on the other side of the wall. We were both deep sleepers, and usually nothing disturbed us.

The quiet when I first awoke was the quiet of an empty apartment. Bertie and Dad had been at work for hours. The sun was bright and warm coming through our big windows facing Main Street.

I laced up my white Keds sneakers, buttoned my shorts and sleeveless blouse, ran a brush through my hair, and headed for the kitchen.

The kitchen door was always open, with the screen door on the back porch locked and bolted. I felt safe and secure as I ate my toast with jelly and drank my icy cold milk, sitting on the screened porch in one of the green-and-white glider chairs.

As I glided and ate, the birds called to one another from their perches high in the stately trees of Miss Nancy's garden next door. Butterflies lighted on the iron railing of the fire escape. The heat off the old tar roof rose in steamy streams, the odor of hot coal and melting petroleum drifting in through the screened porch.

Summer was a time for forgetting about school, a time for leisurely, unsupervised days. The only decision Mikey and I had to make was which swimming pool to walk to that day. But summer did have one rule. Vacation Bible School was a requirement. It was held in our church basement and lasted two weeks. To my brother and me, these were the longest two weeks of summer.

We would play hard all day, then head over to Bible School after supper, freshly bathed, with the grime removed from the bottoms of our feet.

After going barefoot all day, my summer sandals surely did pinch as we walked the three blocks to church. Once we were there, it wasn't that bad. The basement of the church was cool on hot summer evenings. Halfway through class, the teachers served a snack of cookies and lemonade. And the Bible stories were fun.

It was just thinking about it all day that made it seem unpleasant. We would rather go back out and play after supper than go to church. But it wasn't negotiable.

Night after night for two long weeks, Mikey and I were there. Poignantly, Joseph and his coat of many colors still means summer to me.

Summer had its own sounds, smells, and unstructured days. Summer also had its own food. For miles around our lush Cumberland Valley, the farmers' fields burst with crops of sweet corn, tomatoes, peaches, lettuce, and cucumbers. All summer long, Bertie served supper on the back porch. We didn't mind the heat, not with the big fan sitting off to one side and stirring the air.

Picture-perfect strawberries were generously sugared and piled high atop warm homemade biscuits, then covered in cold milk. Roastin' ears from Uncle Leroy's fields were slathered with creamy butter and salt. Lettuce fresh from the farm stand was creamed with sweet-and-sour dressing and slices of hard-boiled eggs. Iced tea was brewed from scratch and served in tall glasses with sugar and lemon. Juice from peaches just plucked ran down our arms as we enjoyed the incomparable sweetness. Some of the peaches were canned quickly and put in the pantry for fresh peach pie in the cold winter months to come.

Summer. Summer in a small town. Summer on Main Street. Everything seemed more clarified. Reality was suspended in the pure essence of carefree days, uncomplicated stories from the Bible, and rich abundance from fields, orchards, and church basements.

Learning the Hard Way

Clack, clack, clack went the sound of my new school shoes with their plastic heels that first week of September in fifth grade. I got the shoes at the five and dime where Bertie worked. She, Dad and Mom saved all year so Mikey and I could have new clothes at the start of the school year. My brother always got a couple of pairs of corduroy trousers, a couple of shirts and shoes. I always got dresses, a cardigan sweater, and black-and-white saddle shoes.

Well, by fifth grade, I was awfully tired of black-and-white saddle shoes, and I pleaded for a change.

I saw them on the rack next to all the saddle shoes: gray "suede" penny loafers, with black heels. Not real suede, but a good facsimile. I fell in love with them.

I was back at my old school with my old classmates. Happy to be in my comfort zone.

Then it happened.

I clacked to the milk cart, got my chocolate milk and straw, and clacked cheerfully back toward the classroom.

"Bonnie Gentry! You come here!"

My teacher's voice froze me in my tracks. Scarlet-cheeked and full of dread, I headed back to the teacher, whom we all knew was strict. She stood near the milk cart, unsmiling and looking unhappy. I began to tremble.

In a stern voice, she said, "You walk back to the classroom on your tiptoes and *stop* smacking your heels on the floor."

My stomach heaved and I thought I might throw up right there. I felt humiliated. I turned and tiptoed back. The only sound was the creaking of the old wooden floor. The students stared at me as I walked on my toes the length of the hallway, through the classroom door, and to my seat.

I felt the pity of many of my classmates, along with the disgust of a few. I wanted to die. I sank into my chair, cheeks burning. What was wrong with me? Why didn't I just stick to those saddle shoes with their softer heel?

I felt a sick uneasiness wash over me. It was going to be a hard year.

Before long, another incident confirmed my fear.

It happened in art class. It was the last period of the day, and we were cutting and pasting crepe paper shapes together. I was seated at the very front of the class, and the teacher placed the large jar of paste on my desk. Inside the jar was a long dipping stick.

I didn't give that jar much thought except that its bulkiness crowded my project. I loved art class and always got lost in my work. I didn't notice the mess my classmates were making as they made trip after trip to my desk to dip out their paste.

When the dismissal bell was about to ring, the teacher said to hurry and clean up our projects before we left for the day.

I put my materials away and neatly folded my own paper creation to carry home in my book.

The bell rang and we all began to head out the door.

"Bonnie Gentry!"

Oh! Just like the last time.

"Bonnie Gentry, you not did clean up your mess."

My throat tightened. As I turned around, I braced for my teacher's scolding. The scolding never came but her body language communicated her displeasure. I walked back toward her. Smeared from top to bottom, inside and out, there it sat: the paste jar, now a total mess. Evidently, my mess to clean up.

I quickly stabbed at the sticky goo with a tissue, but it was way too smeared for that to do any good. She waved me away angrily and began scrubbing at the paste herself. I hung around, hoping to make it better. But she was upset and annoyed, and my attempt to help only made the situation worse.

I slunk out the door and joined my friends, who were waiting to walk home. I poured my heart out to them as we walked. I had lots of excuses. How it wasn't my fault. How I had put my materials away. How everyone else was so messy. I was nauseated, my hands were shaking, and my legs were like rubber.

It was even worse than I thought.

The teacher stomped past us, her gloved hands jammed into her winter-coat pockets. She had missed her ride and had to walk home through the winter cold.

I blamed myself. I had caused this to happen to her. I was insensitive.

That night, filled with self-contempt, I left my art project in the pages of my book, ashamed to show it to my family.

I hated fifth grade.

It didn't comfort me that a classmate was punished and had to sit on the floor for hours because he dropped his pencil once too often, or another ordered to sit on the floor for chatting to her neighbor. Our teacher was not cruel, but her discipline seemed harsh.

Some of the best teachers are strict. I did have other strict teachers. A little discipline didn't hurt any of us. It taught us to be responsible. But this teacher's form of reproof hurt. It was in the way it was delivered: without love, with anger, and with no counterbalancing notice of our good behaviors.

Then one day, a new student arrived, and our teacher smiled. Debbie was intellectually gifted and was placed in our class mid-year. It was apparent that her superior intelligence was far beyond her fourth-grade studies, so she was promoted into our fifth-grade class. Our teacher had been selected to teach this gifted young person, and she beamed when Debbie arrived.

Debbie sat at an oversized desk in the back of our classroom, where she "monitored" what the rest of us were learning. Throughout the day, our teacher talked with Debbie about her assignments. Debbie always finished way earlier than any of us and waited quietly while we completed our work.

The contrast was stunning between the way some of us were treated and the way Debbie was treated.

But Debbie was easy to love. She was smart and obedient. Others of us needed a little more time for our gifts to be revealed.

The sweet spot—that special dimension of unique gifts that exists in each of us—was hidden from our teacher's view and took extra work to develop. Calm, loving guidance works wonders in revealing the unrecognized talents in each of us.

It was a hard year, but I made it through fifth grade. I knew I hadn't measured up to my teacher's standards. I needed to do better.

That summer, I thought of the next school year with gloom.

Little did I know that joy awaited me just around the corner of this long summer.

Mr. Corkle

All summer long, I felt unworthy, humiliated by my poor performance in fifth grade. A heavy, thick, self-loathing rose to the surface like a sharp needle stuck through my peace.

Lazy days of summer, always anticipated, now stretched out endlessly as I contemplated the coming year. As it drew closer, my heart sank a little more each day.

Then at the end of this long, depressing summer, Mr. Corkle received me and my classmates into his lighthearted style of teaching.

He had one of the loudest sneezes I'd ever heard. It exploded like the jolting sound of a truck backfiring. My startled screams finally led him to ring a little bell prior to the next explosion. He even joked about his loud sneezes.

Mr. Corkle had a rich head of hair and kind eyes. He was tall and slim. Years later, I would see a distinct resemblance in Mr. Corkle to President Kennedy. Unwilling to take himself too seriously, he always had a ready laugh and an engaging manner. Informal and open, he often sat on a vacant student desk in the front of the classroom while he taught. Instead of standing over us, he got on our level so he could better engage us in learning.

But although he was fun-loving, he had his boundaries. If you crossed them, you knew swiftly and decisively—yet without feeling like you were wrong or bad. Though he was no one's fool, he had a genuine kindness in his heart for us.

With my self-esteem restored, I relaxed and blossomed in Mr. Corkle's care. He always had time for us and took a real interest in finding the goodness inside each of us. God knew, I needed Mr. Corkle.

I responded with lighthearted give-and-take myself, decent grades, and model behavior. Mr. Corkle brought out the best in me. He renewed my belief in myself.

A year or so later, I saw Mr. Corkle at the community swimming pool where he took a summer job as a lifeguard. True to his boundaries, he scolded and benched me for horsing around in the pool. My embarrassment knew no end. My shame cut me deep. I never wanted to disappoint him.

But I overcame that in time because of how he had made me feel in sixth grade. Worthy, bright, and important.

I never saw him again after that summer at the pool. If only I could tell him the difference he made in my life. He touched my heart with his sincere belief in the sacredness of each young soul.

Friday Nights at the Five and Dime

On Friday nights, an electric charge surged up and down Main Street, starting around four o'clock. That's when the dairy farmers came to town to deposit their milk checks in the bank. Their dusty and worn pickup trucks lined both sides of Main Street, and a hard-working energy crackled in the air.

I loved bumping into my Uncle Leroy as he came down the steps of the bank in his bib overalls, with a big smile and happy to see me. Sometimes, his truck bed was filled with baskets of Silver Queen corn, fresh from his fertile fields. Before heading back to the farm, he always deposited the luscious ears of corn at our front door.

The factory workers came to shop and eat on Friday nights. Burkhart's and The Sugar Bowl restaurants buzzed with the resounding chatter of families enjoying a night out. Mr. Billy, the local cobbler, cranked up his old roaster in front of his shoe store and filled Main Street with the heavenly aroma of freshly roasted peanuts. Store clerks rang sales at cash registers with the merry chinkle of commerce echoing through the streets.

The best part of growing up in a small town, though, was Friday night at the five and dime. I would savor my twenty-five-cent allowance all week in anticipation of walking through every aisle before making my purchase.

The five and dime was organized into sixteen long counters, placed four abreast throughout the store. It was a big store that took up one-quarter of the square on Main Street, filled with hardware, toiletries, sewing notions, and clothing for the entire family.

At the front, the big, glassed-in candy counter brimmed with sugary delights. Chocolate-covered peanuts, orange slices, nonpareils, coconut watermelon slices, candy corn, and gumdrops all waited to be hand-scooped into a bag by the sales clerk.

Next to the candy counter was the cosmetics counter with Tangee rouge, Hazel Bishop lipstick, Pond's cold cream, Camay soap, and clear nail polish. As I got older, I spent more and more time at this counter.

But my favorite counter at the five and dime, where I got lost for hours, was the novelty counter. After browsing the entire store, I lingered there. Trinkets, baubles, and figurines captured my imagination—and most of my allowance. I loved touching all the items and imagined them in my room, or in the corner nook of our living room.

When the ten-minute closing bell sounded for all shoppers to complete their purchases, I finally made my decision from all the choices. One night, a ceramic boy and girl caught my fancy. He was dressed in knickers; she wore a polka-dot dress and carried a gauzy parasol. Another time, it was a set of small ivory vases with rose petals in pale pink and mint green. I was attracted to pretty object d'art priced under twenty-five cents.

Bertie would ring up my purchase and place it in a bag, sometimes wrapping it with extra paper to protect it on our walk home.

Many years later, as I packed up the apartment on Main Street where Bertie and Dad had raised me and had lived for most of their 72-year marriage, I once again touched those trinkets, which still sat in the living-room nook where they had been placed so many years before. I thought how Bertie had carefully wrapped them during those Friday nights at the five and dime. That was a time when decisions were uncomplicated, loved ones were plentiful in my life, and simple, hard-earned energy filled up a small town on Friday nights.

The Library

Essence of mustiness from old leather books, the creaky sound of oiled oak after years of footsteps, and light resembling soft candlelight in an old room at dusk—these were the sights and smells of our public library.

It was housed in a majestic, multistory Georgian Revival-style mansion with a slate-tile roof. The hand-carved railing on the staircase was made of American walnut, with heavy walnut and cherry woodwork throughout the house. Fireplaces with marble mantels and intricately carved moldings, softly glowing chandeliers, gas wall sconces, and Palladian arches exhibited elegance and tastefulness. Finessed with a sensibility and discernment, the sophisticated home was not overdone. There might have been more exquisite places on earth, but not to me. The library was where I could dream big dreams as I envisioned life in such a grand residence.

This impressive structure was the former home of George H. Stewart, Jr., and Dorothy Gray Stewart. After George's passing, his widow Dorothy sold the mansion, for a fraction of its value, to the library organization for its permanent home.

Although George Stewart's brother, Dr. Alexander Stewart, lived right across the street from us, I didn't know the Stewarts. Our lives had entwined only on one occasion, a hot summer day when Mikey and I were walking to the public swimming pool. We were perspiring and sticky when the nice car pulled up at the curb, and an older gentleman rolled down the window and offered us a ride.

Knowing no fear, Mikey didn't hesitate and immediately jumped into the front seat of the stranger's car.

I *did* hesitate. But my brother was already seated and talking his head off to the affable fellow. So I shrugged off my fear and climbed in alongside him.

A bumble bee had taken up residence in the car's front window, and the soft-spoken man asked us to keep an eye on it for him while he drove us to the pool. This heightened my suspicion of the stranger. I was glad when we made it to our destination safe and sound.

I needn't have worried, though. He was just being his kind self.

Only later did I learn that the cordial gentleman was our neighbor Doctor Stewart. The prominent Stewarts did not flaunt their wealth, preferring to carry on their lives unpretentiously. They were highly educated, however, at private academies and prestigious universities, such as Princeton and Washington and Jefferson. The middle names of this large and prosperous clan were often last names of family members, and first names were handed down recurrently through the generations. This naming tradition bestowed an air of decorum to their very presence, despite their preference for understatement. Their prosperity and community spirit had graced the lives of the regular townspeople through their distinguished homes, lush gardens, and contributions to civic causes. And now one of their grandest homes had been repurposed into the public library.

After selecting a book, I would browse the rooms and let my eyes feast on the details of the magnificent home. Impressive rooms with tall ceilings; aesthetically tasteful fireplaces handcrafted with molded plaster designs of rosettes and swags; and oak floors with walnut borders were now recast as reading rooms, outfitted with tables and chairs. The wooden boxes of the card catalog system, situated in each room, did not detract from the floor-to-ceiling refinement.

Out the side door of the mansion and up a few steps was a wide and spacious flagstone terrace. It was now empty and forgotten, but I imagined it once had been filled with wrought-iron tables and chairs. I could see members of the family celebrating their abundant life in the peaceful outdoor setting, while the gurgling Branch Creek flowed close by.

Glorious gardens had once surrounded the terrace on both sides. Now, only a smattering of roses clung to the garden wall, as neglected climbing vines and struggling hedges reached for the sun.

Back inside, I could visualize Mr. and Mrs. Stewart still sitting after dinner in one of the cozy rooms that faced Main Street. Both with their books, perhaps she also with her knitting needles and ball of yarn on her lap. The room would be lit by the soft glow of the gas wall sconces, a fire would be crackling in the fireplace, and every now and then they would look up and exchange pleasantries of the day.

Such, I dreamed, was the life of the genteel and well-to-do. And all these years later, their books and many others lined the walls of each room and inspired seekers of knowledge to make their own dreams come true.

I recently returned to the library and breathed in the nostalgic mustiness once again. Or maybe I was reliving a fond memory. Although the now-modern library boasted the latest in technology, the grand home still inspires generations of hearts to reach their dreams through learning. The Stewarts foreordained that with their gracious gift.

Tucker

When I was twelve, I met Tucker, the college boy, the ideal college boy.

Miss Nancy, who lived right next door to our apartment building, took on a couple of boarders from time to time. With her huge home, she had plenty of room.

Tucker came to board during his senior year of college. Polished and polite, he stood out with his short crew cut, navy suits, white shirts, and ramrod-straight posture.

I wondered where he was from. Maybe he was the grandson of one of Miss Nancy's wealthy roommates from Smith College in Massachusetts. All I knew for sure was that he looked well-off. He carried himself in a stately way that signaled a graceful lineage.

Tucker was so unlike anyone else I had known. From my first glance, I adored him.

Whenever Tucker saw Bertie and me on the street, he would stop and talk. Sometimes, he was out and about with Miss Nancy.

He was seriously charming and had a way of engaging everyone around him. Miss Nancy laughed and lightened her dignified reserve when she was with him.

Then one day, my adoration for Tucker turned to mistrust. From that moment on, I avoided all contact with him. On that day, as usual, he had stopped to talk with Bertie and me. He greeted her warmly, then said to me, "And there's my girlfriend."

My stomach lurched at the word. Girlfriend?

Alarm bells went off. By age twelve, I had built a web of fears from stark memories of things that had happened in the past. From the land-lady in Nashville who had shockingly thrown our kitten over the fence, to Rachel whose reputation was larger than life, to news reports of families losing everything they owned in fires, I had built a big old web of fears. Tucker charmingly and innocently walked into my web.

At his words that day with Bertie, I ducked my head and turned away. I wouldn't make eye contact with this man who now scared me. Was he someone who tried to hurt little girls?

I feared his words meant way more than an offhand comment. No matter how much Bertie prodded me to speak to him, I just couldn't look up at Tucker. I remained paralyzed, frozen in fear.

For the rest of that year, I never connected with him again. At the mere sight of him coming down the street, I avoided him by ducking into doorways and running up the stairs to our apartment. I avoided Tucker and ran from him, much like I had from Rachel earlier.

Because of my unfounded fears, I gave him up as a friend. He left town after graduation, and I never saw him again.

My friend Tucker was on the other side of that fear. My joy was on the other side of that fear.

High-School Years

Beach Party

The Beach Boys, Gidget, and other early 1960s influences gave Mom the idea for my beach party. We would hold it at Laurel Lake in Pine Grove Furnace twenty miles away. As a recently minted teenager that summer of 1962, Mom thought the party fitting for my age group of thirteen- and fourteen-year-olds.

Pine Grove Furnace was a natural and rustically beautiful mountain getaway. The original furnace had been built around 1770 to produce colonial cast-iron products, such as wagon-wheel iron and locomotive parts. Iron production ended in 1895, and the land was sold to the state's parks bureau to become the Pine Grove Furnace State Park in 1931. Laurel Lake was used to transport iron ore and supplies between production facilities, then was restored for recreational use.

"The Lake," as it was known locally, is a twenty-five-acre body of water, surrounded by a lush mountain backdrop and a fairly impressive lakeside beach. Early each morning, while the mist still hovered over the water, tractors raked and groomed the thick sand for the sunbathers who would while away the day. Lifeguards were on duty from morning until sunset.

Picnic tables were scattered among the tall pines, and a snack bar cooked up delicious french fries and cheeseburgers. Hikers on the Appalachian Trail would stop by for a quick lunch and maybe an even quicker swim in the cool water before returning to the trails.

Mom planned my party for weeks. Always erring on the side of generosity, she told me to invite as many friends as I wished; the more the merrier.

As I set out to put my guest list together, I found myself struggling with just whom to put on that list. After all, this wasn't just any party. This was a hip, fashionable party. No other mom had dreamed up such an event for her daughter.

I thought back to fourth grade and those moneyed kids with whom I had rubbed elbows. I so wanted to be good enough for them. We were now rejoined in the junior high school, but we didn't hang out together. This party would show them I was good enough to be their friend. Yes. They were the kids who would make the top of my list, along with a couple of regular kids. I didn't stop to think that I barely knew any of them. That wasn't a consideration as I presented to each of them a personalized invitation to the party of the year.

Mom saved her tip money for weeks to afford the ground beef for the hamburgers she would cook on one of the open grills the park service provided. The dill pickles, large bags of potato chips, soft drinks, potato salad, and hamburger buns all had to be budgeted. Then the paper plates and plastic eating utensils, along with paper cups and napkins. It was a costly party for Mom.

She thought they were my friends. She was thrilled when so many accepted my invitation and said they would attend.

On the day of the party, clouds rolled in, accompanied by a steep drop in temperature. As we loaded up the car with all the food and supplies, I almost began to cry for fear of being rained out. But not Mom. She put a smile on her face and continued to load the car, as if it were a beautiful, warm, sunny day. She encouraged me to smile, too. And she told me not to worry, that all would be fine.

So off we went for our twenty-mile drive to Pine Grove Furnace and The Lake. Mom's friend Joanie came with us to help prepare the food for the crowd of hungry teenagers.

The rain threatened all day, and dark clouds hung like grouchy spoil-sports over the beach and water. Despite the undesirable weather, however, most of the kids did come to my party, driven there in carpools by various parents. They huddled together on beach towels, and wrapped sweaters and shirts around their bathing suits. Only a few ventured into the cold water.

While Mom and Joanie set up picnic tables, cooked hamburgers, and served iced soft drinks, I visited with each person who had come. Briefly visited. I soon ran out of things to say, as we had little in common. Mostly, I stayed off by myself on a separate beach towel, or hung out with one of the regular kids I had invited.

No one was rude. In fact, everyone was polite and mannerly. But we didn't have anything mutually appealing to talk about. They all had much to say to one another and grouped together in quiet, private conversations. Every now and then, one of them looked my way and smiled, but it was awkward for all of us.

After lunch, everyone loaded back up in their respective carpools. With polite and well-mannered words of thanks, they were gone.

Mom was upbeat. "Wasn't it wonderful they all came?" "Weren't they all so nice?" "Did you have a good time?" Finally, "What's the matter, honey?"

Tears stung my eyes and clutched at my throat. What was the matter? I didn't fit in! I wasn't good enough for these kids. I couldn't relax and enjoy myself. It was a disaster.

Yet Mom believed otherwise. To her, I belonged with the best of them.

The problem that day was not the other kids. They couldn't have been more polite. The problem was me.

By separating myself from my own authenticity, I reinforced my belief that I wasn't good enough. I had started out hoping I could be something I wasn't, when all I really needed to do was rest in the simplicity of who I was.

The Princess

The Princess came in soft shades of rose pink, aqua blue, light beige, and snowy white. Her rotary dial lit up every time I used her. Even the ads made her appealing: She was "little." She was "lovely." Most of all, she was *mine*. "To each her own Princess," exclaimed the ad.

I got her as a birthday gift from Mom. I was fourteen, and talking on the phone was my new pastime. I spent hours on the phone with girlfriends, exhausting every teenage topic imaginable. We only hung up when we ran out of breath or someone else needed to use the party line.

Because she was a Princess, I felt like a princess in her presence. Sitting on my nightstand, her graceful lines dressed up my bedroom.

When I made a phone call, I imagined I looked like Doris Day holding a pastel phone in her hand in *Pillow Talk,* as she and Rock Hudson talked endlessly on their party line. Even though I didn't have a Rock Hudson on the other end of the phone, I felt pretty, like Doris, every time I held the Princess to my ear.

I loved that phone. Mostly, I loved that she made me feel special. Mom had sacrificed to get her for me. She didn't lease her; she had bought my Princess outright so she would truly be mine.

Then one day, many years later, I lost her.

I had grown up and moved to my own apartment. By now my Princess was outdated with her rotary dial, so I left her in my bedroom when I moved out. I knew in my heart someday I would reclaim her as a cherished keepsake. The problem was I didn't make that clear to Bertie and Dad.

They had converted my old bedroom into a sitting room and wanted to upgrade the phone to the latest push-button model. The telephone man installed the new phone, disconnected the Princess, scooped her up and took her away. He didn't know she was bought and paid for, and not leased from the phone company. By then, Bertie and Dad had forgotten that part, too.

My Princess was gone, and my attempts to recover her were in vain.

My Princess will forever live in my heart as a symbol of my mom's love and sacrifice for me. To this day, whenever I see a snowy white Princess phone, I get a lump in my throat.

Light and Lasting Touch

"Miss Gentry!" boomed a baritone voice as I walked through the hall of the high school my first year. Classes were changing, and teenagers were milling about everywhere.

I turned and found myself peering up at the impressively tall Mr. Swinsick, the new high school principal. He already knew my name. School had been in session only two days.

It was my skirts. My very short skirts.

"Miss Gentry," he said again, a little less loudly as he towered above me.

I looked up at him anxiously, awaiting what was next.

"Your skirt is too short. I want it down by three inches tomorrow. Is that understood?"

By now, all the kids changing classes had stopped to gawk.

"Yes," I said quietly, but defiantly, then turned on my heel and flounced off. *Yeah, right,* I thought.

For the next couple of weeks, I continued to roll up my skirts, as short as I wanted. I longed to be in style. Truthfully, I really longed to be attractive to all the cool boys in the senior high school. At fourteen, I was desperately seeking attention and approval.

"Miss Gentry." That baritone voice again, a little softer. "I told you to lower your skirts. Now I'm telling you, if you don't, I will send you home next time to change. Is that clear?"

"Yes." I turned and hurried away. This time, I knew he meant business.

However, as was my custom, I continued to roll up my skirts in the hallway outside my apartment each morning before I headed to school.

The third time, there was no fourth time. "Miss Gentry, come here," he said, in a measured, stern voice. "You are to go home, change your skirt to a longer one, and return to class this afternoon. Is that understood?"

"But I will have to walk over a mile," I protested.

"You should have thought about that when I warned you the last time. Go home and change."

I balked. How dare he. Who did he think he was? My skirts were only a little shorter than the other girls, I told myself, untruthfully.

But I did walk home. As I rummaged through my clothes closet under the attic steps, I was hit with a dilemma. *All* of my skirts were short. That I rolled them up even shorter was beside the point.

I found one old relic in the back of the closet, put it on, and walked back to school, imagining that I looked like I had raided Grandma's closet.

With my head ducked and cheeks hot with embarrassment, I slipped into my seat to resume my classes. Humiliated and fuming, I sat there unable to think of anything but the mean, old principal.

Then someone was knocking at the classroom door. The teacher answered and motioned me into the hallway. I had been summoned to the principal's office.

Did he have to pour salt on my wound?

I marched to the office, defiant but scared of this big giant who was in charge of our school.

I rapped a smart-alecky knock-knock on his door. I wasn't about to let him see my fear.

He asked me to come in and motioned me to sit in the only other chair in the small office. Then he came out from behind his desk and sat on the corner of it. He folded his arms and, with a gentle voice, explained to me the proprieties of proper dress for a young lady. He spoke without anger, but as a voice of reason on how dressing properly enhances one's self-image and self-respect.

He made it clear I was not unworthy in his eyes. To him, I mattered, despite what I had done. He encouraged me to higher levels of achievement, to focus on my studies and prepare for life.

I sat there listening with half a mind; the other half was fixated on my embarrassment and anger that he had control over me.

He then dismissed me with a light tone and wished me well. I swaggered out and headed back to class, with a frosty determination not to yield to his words. I was proud, rebellious. I wanted to get back at him.

Halloween night provided the perfect way as it was always a big deal in our small town. The Halloween parade was filled with flowery floats adorned with beauty queens throwing kisses, wearing long, billowy gowns and white gloves. Marching bands from our and neighboring towns played their hearts out in the chilly air. Firemen rode on their shiny red trucks, waving to the large crowds who faithfully gathered each year. The nip in the air made for rosy cheeks on babies and thoughts of hot chocolate when the night was over. The mood was festive, with families huddled together to stave off the cold. Even the beauty queens were wrapped in fake furs to stay warm.

This Halloween night, my high school girlfriends and I attended the parade, along with most of the town. We stood chatting about nothing at all, until we noticed, towering above the crowd, the high school principal.

Wouldn't it be fun, someone suggested, to soap his car windows? Then a few laughs and giggles as we waited for the parade to start.

Before we knew it, we were all running behind the bank to the parking lot in search of his little black car.

We found it promptly and gave it a delicious and total soap job. Someone had come prepared. We all joined in and marked his car windows with heavy, thick lines of white soap. We got him, got him good. It was exhilarating.

Late that night, as I lay in bed covered with warm blankets, a jarring thought hit me. What had we done? What if someone saw us? What if someone told on us?

He had power over us.

He could inform our parents, make us attend extra hours of study hall, blemish our records, kick us out of school. I had never considered the consequences as I gleefully and self-righteously soaped his car.

I finally drifted into a worried sleep and remained concerned the next few days of school. But all was quiet. Not a word was mentioned about our foolish deed.

Until Friday.

I was dressed in a wraparound black skirt and simple blouse. By now, my skirts were a little longer, not that I cared for them. I was beginning to relax a little and began to believe we had escaped unnoticed.

I was wrong.

At the start of study hall and the final period of the day, one by one, my girlfriends and I were summoned to the principal's office.

When every single one of us had arrived, Mr. Swinsick stood quietly, arms folded, with a mischievous twinkle in his eye. Then he told us to follow him.

We looked at each other, wide-eyed. What in the world?

We silently followed his long strides, through the hall to a destination unknown.

He led us to a little-used outdoor courtyard, which was surrounded by classrooms with lots and lots of windows. He held open the double door leading outside, while each of us passed through it.

There, in the center of the courtyard, in all its soapy glory, was his little black car. The soap was still thick and heavy. He had only scraped off enough to see through the front windshield.

It was cold outside that day, and the wind blew right through us. My wraparound skirt flapped in the strong breeze, exposing my thin, white slip.

"Ladies, I believe you know what to do."

With that, he was gone, to the comfort of the warm heat inside the building.

Surrounding the car were buckets filled with water, some with suds, some clear to rinse, plus cleaning rags.

By now, half the kids in school were hanging out windows. No study hall today. Instead, an ethics class in real time.

We cleaned his car, not only the windows, all of it. It took the entire period. As we worked, the five of us confided our shame to each other, worked some more, and began feeling less cold with each stroke of our cleaning cloths.

Then we began laughing. First, with each other. Then with the kids who were hanging out the windows watching us work. Then with Mr. Swinsick, who reappeared to inspect our job. Everyone was laughing.

He took his time walking around his now shiny little black car, savoring the moment with gentle amusement. "Well done. Now you can go inside."

Mr. Swinsick looked for the good in us, even when we disappointed him. He may have wanted to embarrass us a little for our behavior on Halloween night, and he probably wanted some justice. But he cared too much to devalue us or truly punish us for our silly act. He had the power to make it tough on all of us. But he didn't.

Instead, he used a light and lasting touch. The touch of one who is grounded in who he is. The touch of one whose ego doesn't need others to suffer under his power. The touch of one who has a caring soul.

Those Hormonal Years

The streets were dark and deserted at night in my hometown when I was going on 15. In the cold months, folks snuggled in their warm kitchens, enjoying hearty family meals. In the warm months, they gathered in backyards, listening to crickets in the gentle night air.

Nighttime was relaxing family time, for most. Not for me. And not for Cindy, my best friend. She was a year older than me, and we roamed the streets every night without fail. All Bertie and Dad knew was the lie I told them, that I was at Cindy's house each night.

Cindy and I were boy crazy. I had my eye on a senior boy on the wrestling team. He drove an old, fixed-up car and, sometimes, he would drive by as we walked. It thrilled me when he pulled over to the curb and held the door open for both of us to pile into the front seat. My, but it was warm in that car on cold nights.

He knew how young I was, and he already had a girlfriend in a different town. A gentleman, he deposited Cindy safely at her door, then he drove me the extra block to mine.

I had the worst case of puppy love.

For the biggest part of the year, Cindy and I roamed. Sometimes, we visited her granny, which meant we veered off Main Street onto an even darker street. Her granny was elderly and frail but always glad to see us, even though we interrupted her favorite programs on her small black-and-white television. She'd feed us cake, and we would stay about fifteen or twenty minutes. Then we'd leave and roam the streets again.

This went on until an honest boy unwittingly stopped us in our tracks. We were just fooling around one day at my house after school when we decided to call the pay phone next to the Varsity Shoppe. Somehow, we knew the phone number. High school kids went to the Varsity Shoppe after school for grilled cinnamon toast, Cokes, and a game or two of pinball. The jukebox blared, while girls sat in booths carved with lovers' initials and guys sat on round stools at the counter. Then the guys would head outside to hang out on the front steps, right next to the pay phone.

"Hello," said a young male voice the day Cindy and I called. She was on the extension in my dining room at home. I was on my Princess phone in my bedroom, and I laid on the charm in my best pretend voice. I pretended to be "Karen" from Newville, a nearby town with a rival high school. Pure sweetness flowed from my lips through a voice that ran like honey over warm toast. I hooked that young fellow who happened to pick up the phone. He stayed on the phone with us for almost an hour.

When he told us his name, I could not believe our good fortune. He was one of the cutest boys in school. I had never spoken to him, and now I was finding out just how well-mannered he was. On and on we talked.

Then I asked him about certain kids in school: what did he think of this one or that one? He shared his opinions right down the list, all the while thinking he was talking to Karen in another town. Truth be told, he was probably falling for Karen. She was so sweet.

Then I asked him what he thought about Cindy and Bonnie. Did he know them? What were his thoughts about them? Being the upstanding guy he was, he told us. Or he told Karen.

"They're both cute girls," he said. Then the life-changing words: "But they're streetwalkers."

Streetwalkers? It sounded so dirty, so nasty, nothing he wanted any part of.

Immediately, Cindy laid down the extension phone and rushed into my bedroom. We looked at each other, aghast.

The fun was over. The phone call was over. The streetwalking was over. Cindy and I never walked the dark streets again.

And we never thanked the decent boy named Larry, whose truthfulness changed our lives for the better.

Cindy

Cindy was a really cute girl: dark hair, trim figure, just the right amount of freckles. Girls wanted to be part of her inner circle. Boys wanted to date her. She was sixteen now. She was a nice girl, did her homework, and loved to go to the Teen Canteen.

And Cindy loved Ronnie. Ronnie was a senior, and Cindy's guy. She wore his ring around her neck on a long chain, and they dated most Saturday nights.

Cindy and I talked about almost everything under the sun. Makeup, hair, boys. We covered it all.

Over the two years of our friendship, Cindy and I bonded in a special way that made us practically inseparable. Not a day went by that we didn't see each other, walk or ride to school together, or have our talks.

Little did we know that the friendship so dear to both of us would be cut painfully short.

We had just left the Teen Canteen. It was Easter time, and the Canteen was holding a bunny hop that night. Ronnie was busy and couldn't attend the dance, so Cindy and I went together and joined up with a couple of girlfriends.

It was a night like most others at the Teen Canteen, with one exception. On this night, one of the best-looking boys I had ever seen was visiting from another high school about ten miles away. His name was Steve, and he was smitten with Cindy. When they saw each other, sparks flew.

Steve was over six feet tall, blond, lean, and athletic. Any girl would have had a hard time resisting him. He kept asking Cindy to dance, and she kept accepting. Between dances, she expressed her angst to me. After all, she was supposed to be in love with Ronnie.

And she was in love with Ronnie, except that Steve had a certain something she found irresistible. She wrestled with the betrayal all night.

Toward the close of the evening, in a darkened corner of the skating rink where the Teen Canteen was held, Cindy was leaning against a counter, drinking a bottle of soda. She was alone and motioned me over.

"Steve asked to take me home," she said. "I don't know what to do."

Shortly, Steve came over for her answer. She told him quietly that, no, she was going home with her girlfriends. She chose to be true to Ronnie.

Steve left, and the four of us girls piled into Grace's old station wagon. We rode through town on the usual teenage route, from one end of Main Street to the other, where we turned around and repeated the loop all over again.

Shortly, we realized we had a problem. We were getting low on gas.

The only gas station open at that hour was in a remote area on the outskirts of town, so we headed there.

Except—I had a curfew.

I thought about breaking my pesky old curfew as we continued down Main Street. After all, I was fifteen now, and none of my friends had curfews.

"I think I'll just break it tonight," I said, with more than a twinge of defiance.

As we were nearing the door of my apartment building, suddenly my senses returned, or fear set in, or both. Stodgy rule or not, I needed to obey my parents.

"Stop the car," I said firmly. "I need to get out."

That was the last time I saw Cindy alive.

About seven the next morning, Dad knocked on my bedroom door. His face was twisted in pain, and his hand shook as he read from a torn piece of paper from his brown lunch bag.

"Cindy Brown killed. Two other girls critical." His voice quivered.

After hearing the news of the accident on the radio, he had rushed home from work hoping and praying that his own girl was safe in her room. I had gotten out of the car less than thirty minutes before it happened. All because of the curfew.

At the funeral of my lovely friend and due to her significant injuries, a net was placed over the casket so that not even her mother could touch her one last time. Cindy was dead, at sixteen.

For many years, her mother told me how it hurt to see me, knowing we were best friends. But then she would say how pleased she was for our friendship. Others close to Ronnie told me he had many long, lonely nights of falling asleep with Cindy's framed photograph lying on his chest.

Cindy and I were as close as any two friends could ever be. I lost a piece of myself the night she died. It was one of the most tragic events of my life.

Yet, not in vain. Cindy had touched me and others deeply. Her memory will always be alive in my heart as I reflect on the true bond of friendship we shared. Eventually, I applied myself in new ways out of respect for the heartbreaking loss of my cherished friend

It Took a Teacher

Cindy died in March of my sophomore year in high school. Her death had been a sobering wake-up call. Life would take on a deeper meaning for me, and a lot more substance. I was about to grow up.

Only, I had not yet realized it. I was in a bit of a fog.

As I sat doodling in study hall during the last month of that school year, the football coach, who was the room monitor, said to me, "You need to marry a sugar daddy. You're not going to amount to anything."

As it turned out, he couldn't have been more wrong. But at the time, he was more right than wrong.

I had bounced through the early years of high school on a cloud of airheaded nonsense, unfocused and undisciplined. Skirts too short, study habits poor, full of know-it-all opinions.

I was on a misguided course to nowhere. I knew things had to change.

That following September after the football coach pronounced his opinion of my future, I met the teacher who changed the course of my life.

Kind, disciplined and down-to-business, Mrs. Marguerite Jacobs worked us hard in her class.

She taught Gregg shorthand, a marketable and coveted skill. I took to it like a duck to water. Challenged by this fascinating communication form that demanded speed, precision and order, I was Mrs. Jacobs' top student for both my junior and senior years of high school, and ultimately, set a school record.

An observant teacher, Mrs. Jacobs saw in me a native intelligence that others had missed. She nourished it with a belief that even I began to trust.

I can imagine how she must have had to defend her faith in me to her colleagues in the teachers' lounge. Everyone thought I was an airhead. But defend me, she did. Have faith in me, she did. Her confidence cascaded into my other studies, and I began to excel in school.

Gentle Giant

My brother preferred to be called Mike instead of Mikey when he became eleven or twelve years old. By then, it was clear that Mike valued harmony above any ego need to look and act tough. To him, harmony was about showing respect for others and about bringing a calm influence into any interaction. He never sewed discord and rarely got angry.

Mike was a big boy, tall and sturdy. He could have easily defended himself in a scuffle. It just wasn't in him to fuss and fight. With his gentle nature, he walked away from a disagreement to preserve the harmony he valued.

Word got out: "Gentry doesn't fight."

For this reason, Mike was continually bullied by other kids.

He stood courageously true to himself, despite what others thought. The bullies didn't see it as courage, particularly when one bully was paired with another bully or even a gang of bullies.

When he was twelve, the paperboys picked on him. The Town Stationery shop was housed on the first floor of our apartment building. Twice a week when our town's newspaper, The News Chronicle, was printed, the paperboys gathered at the foot of our fire escape to organize their newspapers in their bicycle baskets.

Mike often passed by them on his way home from school. Routinely, a couple of boys would heckle and punch him. Mike just pushed through them and came up the steps to our apartment. This taunting and punching went on for the better part of a year.

When I heard the commotion going on Down Back, I knew it meant the paperboys were at it again with my younger brother. With my long legs and arms flailing, I would race down the steps, scold the paperboys, and stand there until they quit. Then I'd scold them some more as I walked back up the stairs. They grumbled and yelled ugly things at me, but I didn't care.

Then when he turned thirteen, six or seven boys ganged up on Mike on his way home from school. They rushed him, pushed him against a wall, and forced him to eat ants. As some of the boys held his arms and legs, the other boys shoved the live ants into his mouth. A small group of kids stood by watching. The bullies laughed when tears came into Mike's eyes. They mocked him and called him a baby.

As was Mike's way, he didn't say a word about the bullying to anyone in the family. Just as when he was a little boy, Mike bore his pain alone. When I heard about it from some classmates, my heart hurt for him. I'll never know who the boys were who had shown such cruelty.

Then one day, the bullying stopped. Mike didn't say, but I believe the ants-episode had a lot to do with it. He didn't fight. He didn't betray his gentle nature. He just refused to be stepped on any longer. With his resolute mindset, he stood down his bullies. No one ever pushed him around again.

Mike's affinity for harmony lasted all his life. It was his greatest strength.

Birth of a Tinker Bell

I was almost sixteen, enormously peer-conscious, and at thirty-nine, my mother was pregnant. I wanted to die. Moreover, I wanted nothing to do with that child.

She and my stepfather Woody seemed happy, but I hadn't bargained on a child entering the picture a year into their marriage. Why couldn't she be content with just my brother and me? Why would she even want a child at such an advanced age?

Her awfully pregnant stomach was more than I could bear. How could she be so overjoyed when I was so miserable? And when she rubbed coconut oil all over her bulging tummy to help with the stretch marks, I thought I would suffocate.

In some of Mom's darkest days in the years before, she didn't realize she was giving Mike and me up forever to Bertie and Dad. She felt we were on loan until she could get on her feet. Then time, familiarity, and circumstances took over, and she lost us. Mom was never able to reclaim us again as solely her own. She must have suffered deep sadness over that stark truth.

Out of respect for Bertie and Dad, Mom stepped into the shadows and permitted them to raise us as they saw fit. She trusted their good hearts. Mom stayed close to us and was involved in our lives. But she couldn't be the mother she longed to be.

Now she had found a new love, and they were pregnant. Finally, she would have a child of her own.

During the long months of her pregnancy, I was angry with my mother. Angry, hurt, resentful. Her love and loving ways were now going to be given to someone I didn't know, someone else who would get all the attention, someone who could take my place.

This drove me to nasty behaviors any time I was in my mother's presence. I mouthed off and vowed repeatedly that I would not love this or any child she had.

She smiled through it all. She did not let my misguided jealousy mar her joy. This unborn child would be her second chance at motherhood.

Then she was born.

In the middle of the night, my stepfather called, "It's a girl."

A tender emotion charged through me that I wasn't expecting. From then on, she was my little sister.

Susan had big blue eyes, chubby cheeks, and a few strands of light brown hair on top of her head. They brought her home to their apartment, where Mom had lived for so many years across the old tar roof from Bertie and Dad's.

One look at that tiny face and little head melted all my resentment. That compact bundle captured my heart.

Mike, now thirteen, picked her up in his arms. She felt so light to him that he nicknamed her Tinker Bell. He adored her.

From the beginning, I had a special connection with my sister. Each day after school, I raced home, slung my books onto the dining room table, and raced across the roof to Mom's apartment. My legs could not take me there fast enough, and my homework would have to wait.

When she was just old enough to stand, Tinker Bell would wait for me at the screen door of Mom's kitchen. With her nose pressed against the screen, she called for "Baw," her attempt at my name.

I loaded her into the stroller, and off we went to the five and dime to visit Bertie, who always stood at her post at the front cash register. My little sister never seemed to mind the rough patch of railroad tracks we had to traverse to cross the town square. She just bounced merrily along, in the security of her big sister's care. Thank God I had lost my oversized teenage ego with its associated nastiness.

But my fears did come true. Tinker Bell did steal Mom's heart. She took a prominent place in my mother's life, and she definitely got most of the attention. Thankfully, my love for her overcame all of that.

One of my sweetest realizations was accepting and celebrating this child whom Mom could call her own, this child she could raise, this child she could watch grow and develop without an arm's length distance separating them.

And something else I celebrated. Mom's huge capacity to love. I was no longer threatened by the fear I would lose her. Her love was big enough for all of us.

And so I gained a sister, and one of life's sweetest treasures.

Red Mustang

Cynthia was seventeen or eighteen, a year ahead of me in high school. Her dad had just married the widow of one of our town's most prominent businessmen. Heads turned when Cynthia drove around town in the new 1965 Mustang her father and stepmother gave her when she became a high school senior. It was sleek and red, with a shine that wouldn't quit. It was eye-popping. And it was all hers.

I thought Cynthia was the luckiest girl on earth. I would lie awake and dream about her life. Since I didn't really know her, I made it up.

I saw her living in a big stone house with a beautiful soft pink bedroom. Not hot pink. Not bubblegum pink. Blush pink, a light pink with just the slightest tinge of brown to add sophistication, adorning her bed in sumptuous waves of covers and oversized fringed pillows. I imagined expensive rugs, richly textured and hand-loomed in blush pink, ivory, pale blue and soft yellow. Everything perfect.

I pictured windows covered in abundant layers of silk curtains tied back with silk sashes. She would have her own stereo system and all the 45-rpm records her heart could desire, from Ricky Nelson to Bobby Vinton. Her closet would be full of cardigan sweater sets in thick cotton and cashmere, penny loafers, and sling-back flats with big bows. I imagined Cynthia doing homework in the soothing quiet of her bedroom, at a desk with curved legs and matching chair.

I couldn't get Cynthia off my mind and marveled at her turn of fortune. It was a Cinderella story, and I lived her fairy tale vicariously in my thoughts each night. A different world from mine.

My windows were covered in curtains from the five and dime, where Bertie had an employee discount. They were always crisp and starched, and showcased the sparkling-clean windows, polished by my cousin Larry. But they weren't made from silk.

My furniture was from Brenner's, whose affordable brands lived in many a home of the hardworking people in town. Neat and tidy, but not heirloom quality.

Our good car was a hand-me-down from Dad's good friend Stoey. It was shined and ready to take us to church each Sunday. A pretty car, but not a new, red Mustang.

I didn't mind the differences all that much, but it sure was fun to imagine Cynthia's dreamy life.

Years later, those musings had faded from my memory. By then, I celebrated my own life growing up with Bertie, Dad and Mom. Mike and I might not have had expensive cars, silk curtains or heirloom furniture, but we had a nurturing home, plenty of food, and unconditional love.

There was nothing else I could have asked for. There was nothing else to take the place of all that.

Laundromat

Every Monday after work, Dad drove off in his old Studebaker with our huge wooden laundry basket filled to the brim with clothes, towels, and bedsheets. He headed to his sister Ethel's house, where she did our laundry from a washer and dryer in the basement of her home. We didn't have a washer or dryer, and Pappy's old wringer washer had played out long ago.

Once Ethel cleaned everything, she neatly folded and stacked all the fresh laundry into the basket for the trip back home. This went on week after week.

Ethel was a good woman and a good sister to Dad. The little money we paid could not have compensated her adequately for the hard work.

Plus, at Christmas time, onto the top of the basket she piled cookies and candy, homemade in her kitchen.

Sometimes I went along to drop off or pick up the laundry. I loved riding in that old Studebaker, with its musty smell and solid work ethic. I especially loved riding through Ethel's neighborhood of Hollar Heights and dreaming of one day owning a nice home like the ones there.

But then came a time when Ethel no longer had to do our laundry. That was when the laundromat came to town. Now Bertie and I could do it ourselves.

Bertie's disability did not defeat her as she and I lugged the stuffed clothes basket down the fire escape of our apartment building, through the rutted dirt parking lot in back, and across the paved public parking lot just beyond. We sat the basket down to catch our breath before crossing the street and heading toward Branch Creek, which flowed alongside the new laundromat.

The laundromat was a sight to behold, with its shiny linoleum floor and long rows of white washers ten deep on both sides, their silver-slotted tongues waiting to be fed a quarter. An equally long row of white dryers stood ready to spin, for ten cents a load. Our small town had finally entered the modern world.

For the next few years, going to the laundromat was an event. I always made sure my nails were done, because I loved pretending I was one of the ladies in a magazine advertisement doing her laundry in style.

I would load the washer, shake the detergent over the clothes, and click the quarter into the slot. Gee, but I felt uptown, with my pretty nails.

While the clothes washed, Bertie would thumb through a magazine or a leftover newspaper. I'd walk outside to Branch Creek and look over the little bridge at the clear water. Fish lived happily and abundantly there. The rhythm of the running stream put me in a trance, absorbed by daydreams. I felt grown up and special.

After I graduated from Shippensburg University and got a good job, I saved enough money to purchase a washer and dryer for Bertie and Dad. With barely enough room in the apartment, we found a small spot close to the bathroom for a stackable unit.

No more lugging that stuffed clothes basket down the fire escape and across two parking lots. No more stress and strain on Bertie's tired back. She could do her laundry any time she chose; and she chose to do her laundry every day. She took pleasure in keeping everything fresh.

For more than thirty years, she kept the washer and dryer working like Trojan horses. Somewhere in Pennsylvania today, that stackable washer and dryer are probably still going strong. One thing's for sure; no one could ever appreciate them like Bertie did.

The laundromat is gone now, having grown worn and weary from its public life. But in its day, it was a blessing.

Unlikely Queen

Our local five and dime was a steady feature in my life and even more so when I turned sixteen and began working there. On nights and weekends during my junior and senior years of high school, I worked various counters in the store from candy to hardware to ladies lingerie.

The on-the-job training course taught me and my class of newly hired employees to arrive early, to clean up our counter before leaving for the day, and, above all else, to honor the customer. "The customer is always right," said the trainer. Over and over she drilled into our heads this fundamental principle of the G. C. Murphy Company, our employer.

My favorite place to work was the candy counter. Customers were always in such a good mood when I handed them their sweet selections. Eventually, I followed in Bertie's footsteps and became a cashier.

I was fast on the cash register and shoppers used to marvel at my speed. That was all okay until I started to show off for the small crowds that gathered to watch my handiness with the keys.

To demonstrate my skill, I pushed my fingers even faster than my brain and began to make errors. It didn't take me long to come to my senses and slow down. I was maturing, but I always had to learn the hard way.

While my work life was active during high school, my social life was off to a slow start.

Many of my girlfriends had boyfriends by the time we were in eleventh grade. I didn't. After I got over my mad crush in ninth grade for the senior wrestler, I had little interest in dating. Naïve and finally focused on my grades in my junior year of high school, I spent my spare time either studying or working.

My social life took a step forward in my senior year, however, when three cute boys expressed interest in me. First, there was Ronnie, a tall and charming basketball player. Then, Rick, handsome and sweet. Finally, towards the end of senior year, I got acquainted with Jimmy. Blond and attractive, Jimmy was popular and active in sports.

When Jimmy asked me to the senior prom, I was surprised and excited. Due to arriving late onto the dating scene, I had thought my prospects were low for an invitation to the biggest social event in high school.

As the weeks stretched on to prom night, my anticipation was building. Along with six or seven other couples, Jimmy and I were selected to be on the prom court. How thrilling it all was. Because I had saved my money from working at the five and dime, I was able to buy a soft yellow prom gown. It was sleeveless with a long slim skirt that almost touched the floor. Jimmy was tallish, but I couldn't wear high heels or I would have been taller than him. I settled for a lower heel which looked awfully nice with my gown.

About two weeks in advance of the big night, I asked my work supervisor if I could have prom day off. She took her time thinking about it. In the end, she didn't give me the day off but did give me the night off. Promptly at 5 pm on prom night, I bolted out of the store and raced down the street to our apartment. Jimmy was taking me to a swanky restaurant for dinner about ten miles away. I had only moments to get ready.

Rushing out of my work clothes, I freshened up and threw on my dinner dress. I looked in the mirror and swiped my long hair with a brush. Oh, but my bangs were looking oily this late in the day, and there was no time to wash my hair. I pushed aside my discomfort over my bangs and finished dressing.

Off I went to dinner with Jimmy, now with a brand new concern on my mind. Would I have proper manners for this classy restaurant? Jimmy carried himself well, and he was from a respectable family in town who owned a business and a nice home. I felt insecure as I got into the front seat of his car.

I needn't have worried too much because Jimmy did me a favor during dinner when he accidentally dropped his buttered roll onto his lap. As he turned his eyes toward heaven in good-natured remorse, I felt my own pressure of messing up melt away. I relaxed. A little bit.

After we ate, Jimmy drove me home and then went to his house to get ready for the prom. I changed into my lovely gown, which looked elegant with my new shoes. I touched up my makeup and, once again, brushed my hair. Those bangs! By now, they had separated into greasy strands across my forehead.

If only I had had time earlier today to shampoo my hair, I lamented. Why didn't my supervisor let me off work for the day? Didn't she understand how important a senior prom was? I pushed my angst aside, because there was simply no time for it.

In short order, Jimmy rang the doorbell. When he saw me in my gown, he said I looked nice. He looked dashing in his white dinner jacket, black bow tie, and dress pants. Mom took pictures of us in the living room, while Dad, Bertie, Mike and my little sister Susan watched from the sidelines on the couch.

After pictures and hugs from my family, we left for the prom.

Once we arrived, we mingled in the high school lobby with the other prom-goers, many of them our mutual friends. The class advisor lined up the prom-court couples in a certain order. First, this couple. Then, another couple. Jimmy and I were being steered to the back of the line, and I knew something was up. Then the magic words from the advisor to Jimmy and me: "You two are entering last. The student body has voted you our new prom king and queen."

My heart soared. I couldn't believe it.

In an organized procession, we entered and stood at the back of the gymnasium that no longer resembled its sporty self. A dark and dreamy blue hue created an impression of the night sky. A silvery reflection cast a moonlit glow on the entire room. Roses and twinkling stars completed the shimmering garden setting. I could almost feel the coolness of the mist hovering around us.

Finally, it was time for the prom court to promenade.

As the other couples took turns slowly walking to the front of the room, Jimmy and I waited our turn. When the speaker announced our names as the new king and queen, there were lots of cheers and applause. I was euphoric with the validation of my schoolmates.

As we started to move to the front, Jimmy had to tell me to slow down walking. I was nervous and didn't realize I was practically loping. If only he would have also encouraged me to spit out the gum I was unmindfully chomping.

Now at the front of the room, we took our seats on the two "thrones" that were positioned on a slightly elevated platform covered in synthetic grass. I continued to chew away on my gum while a tall crown made of crepe paper was placed on Jimmy's head. A rhinestone tiara was placed on mine, right on top of those buttery bangs.

After we were crowned, the photographer took pictures for the high school yearbook and The News Chronicle, our town's twice-weekly newspaper. Following the photo session, the class advisor instructed us to step onto the gymnasium floor. As the orchestra played its version of "Ebb Tide," Jimmy and I danced as king and queen.

After that night, Jimmy and I went our separate ways.

As I reflected on the prom in the weeks that followed, I still found it hard to believe that I would be voted anyone's queen. But I was and basked in the warmth of that night for many months. In truth, I didn't know how to act like a queen, but a considerate boy named Jimmy never let on if it bothered him.

Crowning Glory

As I sat there on graduation night, with scholastic awards being presented, recipients' names were called one by one. I watched select members of my class of 200 go forward for their awards. I looked on with admiration, and a little envy. They were the smart kids. In many cases, the well-to-do kids. They excelled, were deserving, and, in all likelihood, were heading to college.

Then my name was called. My heart beat fast. Mrs. Jacobs, the high school teacher who had believed in me, had nominated me for a scholastic award of distinction in the business curriculum.

That validation was the beginning of my earnest desire to go to college. That night, I realized I wanted more. I recognized I could make something of my life.

It took one teacher, one very special teacher. She saw me, and she saw good. Her affirmation gave me the confidence to believe in myself.

One teacher can change everything.

College

Last Reunion

I was twenty-one, and my father had been gone since I was three.

Sometime before seven in the morning, I was jolted awake by the ringing of my Princess phone on the nightstand. I was still living with Bertie and Dad while I finished college.

Who was calling so early, I wondered. Sleepily, I answered, "Hello?"

"Hi, Honey. It's your daddy."

I barely recognized his voice, even with his Southern accent. "Hi, Dad," I said tentatively, with a question in my voice.

"Honey, I've come to see you. I'm at the bus station. Can you come get me?" The bus station was an hour away.

I was headed to campus to take some of my college final exams. At his words, I panicked. "No, Dad. I can't come and get you," I said hurriedly.

There was a pause.

"Oh. OK, Honey. I'll get there somehow."

I hung up on that clear morning in May and knew my life was about to change. I rushed to Bertie's bedroom to tell her the news.

I had loved him all my life. Mom had made sure of it. She always said he was worthy of my love, simply because he was my father. Because of her, I never let him go. When I was young, she had told me all the good things about him. As I got older and pleaded with her to shed more light on who he was, she told me the other side: the drinking, the restlessness, the trauma from the awful war.

I had heard from my father about a half-dozen times while I was growing up. Sometimes, in drying out periods, he penned beautiful letters. During my senior high school years, he called on a few occasions to the principal's office. Someone would come and get me from class and I would talk with my father over the phone for a few moments. I cannot recall a phone call when he had not been drinking.

But, most times, it was as if I didn't have a real father.

And now he was back.

Back. That thought made me a little crazy. Did I even want him back? What did it mean, his coming back? Where would this lead?

I headed to campus in my old black-and-white Ford, with the crumpled fender I couldn't afford to fix, to take my exams. Not that I could concentrate.

Nevertheless, I slugged through the morning tests, all the while fighting a slew of unsettling, piercing emotions.

Through the years, I had felt the pain of my father's absence. It hurt to love him and not have him. His return reopened the wound.

After the morning exams were finished, I headed to the college president's office where I worked as a student secretary. I was explaining why I couldn't come to work later that day when the phone rang. It was for me. It was the operator downstairs in the lobby.

"Bonnie, you need to come down here," she said. "There's a man here who says he's your father."

I suddenly felt like I was in a slow-motion movie. I could hear what everyone was saying but it seemed foggy and surreal. I knew I had entered a special moment in time.

Eventually, I started down the long hall to the winding staircase of Old Main. From the top of the stairs, I could see him sitting on the bench, looking into the eyes of each coed who passed by. He was searching for his daughter.

I wasn't prepared for the sight of him. He looked immaculate and strikingly handsome. He was well-dressed. His coal-black hair was thick, wavy and neat as a pin.

I was halfway down the stairs when he looked into my eyes and stood up. He knew me right off.

It was *his* eyes that really got me. Amber brown, warm, and soft. My father. Johnny.

He began to cry openly, right there in the lobby of Old Main, with all the college kids streaming by. I was so embarrassed, I asked him to step outside with me.

Once away from all the passers-by, he hugged me and cried some more. And he kept on crying all the way to my car, which was parked on a side street.

We got in and I drove to Bertie's. She had anticipated that he would come directly from the bus station to her house later that morning, so she adjusted her shift at the five and dime to be home when he arrived. Instead, he came straight to me.

I was confused and anxious. Yes, he was back. But somehow, I knew, not for good. Johnny was an alcoholic. He had been one since the war.

Bertie was glad to see Johnny. She had always liked him. Everyone did. He was still the mannerly, kind, Southern man she remembered. He also was different.

The years of alcohol abuse had taken their toll. His hands shook, and he was noticeably nervous and jittery. His face bore the stress lines of a life lived hard—and something else. Johnny now had an apologetic way about him, like he felt unworthy, like he knew he had wasted his life.

Bertie noted how thin he was and made him something to eat. But he didn't eat. Said he couldn't. He was too upset at seeing his children and all of us again. Instead, he asked our permission to run "real fast" to the American Legion and get a drink.

That's when *I* cried. "Don't do this, Dad. Not today."

With hands that shook, he explained his illness and his real need for a drink. "Baby, I'm an alcoholic. I must have a drink. You don't understand. I must have a drink." He pleaded with his eyes.

Bertie said, "Honey, you've got to let him go get a drink. He's telling the truth." Like she knew. Like she understood.

Tears streaming down my face, I reluctantly said, "Go ahead. But come right back."

"I'll go real fast, Baby. You'll see. I'll be right back."

I nodded, warily, and he raced down the fire escape, hurried across the dirt parking lot to the alley, and headed the half block to the American Legion.

He was back in a flash. "See, I told you I would be right back." He smiled, in his charming way.

We visited for a good while. Laughing, sometimes crying, and remembering the early years.

"How's your mother?" he wanted to know. "What does your brother look like? Is he tall?" "What are you taking in college?"

We caught up on my life in a matter of a few hours.

Then it was time for me to head back to campus to take more tests. Bertie went back to the five and dime to work the rest of her shift. Mike, now out of high school, was working at his job at the paper company. Dad was at the furniture factory. Mom, by then, had moved to another town with my stepfather and sister.

No one was home to visit with Johnny. So he headed back to the American Legion.

I worried all through my exams. After I finished, I headed home, scared of what I would find.

As soon as I reached the top of the fire escape, I saw Johnny, passed out on the chaise lounge on the back porch. My heart broke at the sight of him lying face down. His beautiful three-piece gray suit was wrinkled and disheveled. When I woke him up, I saw a big crease down the side of his face from where he had been lying. His eyes were bloodshot.

He was drunk, and he just wanted to leave. "Take me to the bus station," he demanded. "I want to go home."

Bertie was back by now and insisted on giving him strong black coffee before we made the forty-mile trip to the bus station. As he was sitting at the kitchen table, sipping the strong coffee and waking up a little, Mike walked in. Now six-foot-four, with black hair and warm amber eyes, he looked like his father.

Johnny stood to his feet and sobbed, "My son. My son."

It must have been so unnatural for Mike. The only father he'd ever known wasn't Johnny. It was our uncle, who had raised us with a father's love and now had joined us at the table.

Mike was distant and uncertain, but polite. He kept swallowing as he watched his real father cry. Meanwhile, he kept stealing glances at Dad to be sure Dad was OK with this. Johnny was a stranger. He'd left when Mike was an infant.

Later, Mike and I helped Johnny into the front seat of Mike's car for the ride to the bus station an hour away. I rode in back.

Johnny was still intoxicated and slept most of the way. Mike and I drove in silence.

As soon as we arrived inside the bus station, Johnny declared in a loud voice that he had to find a bathroom. People stopped and stared.

Mike went with him, unsure what else to do.

While they were gone, agonizing thoughts cut through me. I wanted to break down and cry. I didn't want this for my father. I couldn't bear it for him.

But this was my father, and this was his life. Stared at. Pitied. Looked down on.

An overwhelming sadness filled me. His lovely potential was denied him, buried deep under the veil of his addiction.

They emerged from the restroom, and Johnny headed to the ticket counter. He tried to sign his name on a traveler's check, but it was illegible, and the ticket agent refused it.

She looked at me. "If he can't sign his name, I can't cash this and get his ticket."

I tried to help, but Johnny loudly proclaimed, "John Gentry can sign his own name."

After three failed attempts, the agent took pity on both of us. "OK, Honey. I'll accept this, even though I shouldn't."

Now, with a one-way ticket back to Nashville and two hours to kill, Johnny wanted to go have coffee. Then, the inexplicable hand of God intervened. Johnny sobered up, as if he had never been drinking.

For those two hours before he got on the bus, he was all ours, my brother's and mine.

Johnny and I talked, shared and cried. He said the things he had come all the way north to say. He asked for our forgiveness, expressed love for our mother, and told us over and over how much he loved us.

He pulled out his well-worn wallet to show us a tattered picture he carried everywhere with him. It was the newspaper clipping of me being crowned high school prom queen. How he got it, I'll never know. As I stared down at the clipping, I visualized him pulling it out of his wallet and telling people, "See, I have a daughter. I had a life."

We sat there in the bus station's café with our coffee, lost in time. This was our day with our father. We didn't know it then, but it would be our last day ever with him. Mike sat patiently and quietly listening to what Johnny said. He couldn't share memories because he was so young when our father left. The only thing he could do was show respect to the man whom he so closely resembled.

The boarding call came for Nashville, and we walked Johnny to the bus. Mike carried the suitcase. I wondered about that suitcase and if Johnny had intended to stay longer.

The other passengers had already boarded. Johnny turned, tears streaming down his face. He shook Mike's hand and told him he loved him. Mike cleared his throat and mumbled something under his breath.

Johnny reached out and gave me a vigorous, emotional hug. "I love you, Baby."

I didn't hesitate. As Mom's grace and love shone through me, I said, "I love you, too, Dad." I couldn't see him for my tears, but I know he heard me.

Then he was gone. I cried all the way home.

That dark night, Mike and I drove home in silence. Deep in his own thoughts, he kept looking over at me from time to time, worried.

Johnny died that August. He had chosen alcohol over us, trying to escape a life he couldn't live. But he loved us.

Epilogue

My youth and adolescent years gave me two essential values: determination and work ethic. With the grace of God, these values led me to the mahogany boardrooms of Fortune 100 and 200 corporations where, for thirty-seven years, I progressed up the corporate ladder to the top. Even though I was different from most "corporate types," there was always a CEO who appreciated the unique skills I brought to the table.

Often, I was the only woman in those esteemed rooms. At times, I felt like a fish out of water, as I struggled to feel worthy enough to be there. Other times, I grew weary of the linear side of the corporate world. My head and heart cried out for the spiritual, creative side of business where the focus is more on the people who make corporations great. I was always less concerned with what got done and more concerned with *how* it got done. In other words, who we were being as a corporation when we did the things we did.

I've been blessed with success that, as a child, I never considered attainable. Now I am in the retirement chapter of my life, and there is no sitting around relaxing. This is the time of my life I give back. This book is part of giving back.

I pray that my journey will touch countless numbers of people to find meaning and a way to a better life.

Mom, Bertie and Dad were inspirational role models. They worked hard and loved even harder. They didn't have much, but they gave me everything that was important. They knew that the true meaning of abundance is a child's laughter filling a childless home, rusty rails planted in cement to make a swing set soar, and a pantry full of good food for enthusiastic tummies.

Dad struggled with health issues for many years, due to how hard he pushed himself in the factory and in that old cellar, firing the furnace at all hours of the day and night. But it was Bertie who passed first, while Dad was living in a nursing home. Her silent killer was colon cancer. By the time we knew, it was only a matter of hours until she was gone. When I had to break the news to Dad, with my ever-faithful cousin Larry by my side, tears flooded his eyes and ran down his cheeks. He bowed his head and quietly said, "My sweetheart is gone." He died seven weeks later.

Mom endured two failed marriages but *never* lost her capacity to love. She poured her love into her three children and her large family. We knew something was wrong when she could no longer remember how to put away the groceries. She had Alzheimer's disease, yet she loved us all the way through those eleven torturous years.

Mike grew to be tall and handsome, like his father. Sadly, he followed in his father's steps to war and an early death. He left behind his beloved wife Ellen and beautiful daughter Jessica. He will never be gone as long as his daughter is alive. Their resemblance is a loving reminder of the sweet, gentle soul who was my brother. Jessica and I cherish a deep bond of love.

My baby sister Susan married Sito, her high school sweetheart. They have two sons, my beloved nephews Joshua and Noah. Even though she and I are sixteen years apart in age, we are as close as two peas in a pod. It started the day Mom brought her home from the hospital and I was up to my elbows in suds, washing her baby bottles. Our relationship is kissed by God and Mom.

My rock for over thirty years has been my husband Lee. He's my mentor, my grounding, my Southern gentleman, and my whole heart. His encouragement and trust have inspired me to always reach higher. It is nothing but a pleasure to spend more time with him now. His unconditional love envelops me, and I am blessed beyond my dreams.

My life is not about loss. It is about God's blessings.

Since Bertie rescued me from that sewer drain, God's hand has guided and shaped my life, which is filled with joy.

The one lesson I have learned above all: Joy is within each one of us. We just have to choose it.

Acknowledgments

Wally Bock, whose accomplished scholarship taught me how to write and then write better.

Charles Loucks, whose love and knowledge of history enriched this book with principled accuracy.

The Shippensburg Historical Society, for sharing hard-to-find chronicled data.

About the Author

Bonnie C. Hathcock has over 35 years of experience in corporate America. For most of those years, she held C-suite positions at the top of Fortune 100 and 200 corporations. Bonnie began her career at Xerox Corporation, where she spent a decade learning world-class marketing concepts. Her business and marketing acumen eventually caught the attention of a high-ranking executive from Siemens A.G. who promoted Bonnie to the position of vice president of human resources for one of the largest Siemens corporations in the USA. Bonnie would eventually be promoted to vice president of Human Resources for US Airways and senior vice president of Human Resources for Humana Inc.

Bonnie's work ethic and drive for excellence awarded her the distinction as one of the Top 25 Most Influential Women in Human Resources in 2005. In 2007, Bonnie was named Human Resources Executive of the Year, a national award presented by *HR Executive* magazine. In 2010, Bonnie was inducted as a fellow into the National Academy of Human Resources.

Bonnie has an MBA and has completed post-graduate studies at the Stanford University School of Business. She resides in Tennessee with her husband Lee and Cavalier King Charles Spaniel Cubby.

CPSIA information can be obtained
at www.ICGtesting.com
Printed in the USA
LVOW10s1319301017
554285LV00017B/559/P